A NICE GIRL LIKE ME

A NICE GIRL LIKE ME

The autobiography of Gloria Lovatt

GLORIA LOVATT
AND
PAM COCKERILL

Columbus Books

London

A Nice Girl Like Me is a true account of the life of Gloria Lovatt. However, certain names have been changed for legal reasons.

First published in Great Britain in 1988 by
Columbus Books Limited
19-23 Ludgate Hill, London EC4M 7PD

Copyright © Gloria Lovatt and Pamela Cockerill 1988

British Library Cataloguing in Publication Data
Lovatt, Gloria
  A nice girl like me.
  1. Prostitution
  I. Title   II. Cockerill, Pam
  306.7'42'0924   HQ117

ISBN 0 86287 401 7

Typeset by Facet Film Composing Limited, Leigh-on-Sea, Essex

Printed and bound by Mackays of Chatham Limited

PART 1

1

I was 23 years old when I got the beating-up which broke my ribs and made me think for the first time about giving up prostitution. It was 1974. I'd been on the game in London for about a year, living in a hotel in Sussex Gardens and working from Shepherd Market, a notorious red-light area. It was a good base for picking up clients and I was able to earn quite reasonable money without having to work too hard.

On a typical day I'd spend the morning shopping, eat a good lunch, then, at about 2 o'clock, go back to my hotel room and get dressed for 'business'. My work outfit was quite a sight. I usually wore a black low-cut cocktail dress which I'd bought in Carnaby Street, with black tights, black patent stilettoes, and, to finish off the outfit, a red fox fur. I never wore too much make-up, though. I didn't like to look too obvious, unlike some of the girls on my patch.

So, dressed to kill, I'd get a taxi to Shepherd Market, have a drink in the King's Head and pick up a client – or if I was lucky a regular would find me – and take him back to my hotel room. For £20 he'd get about a quarter of an hour. On a good day I'd have done business with three customers before 6 o'clock and be finished in time to catch the evening show at the cinema.

I wasn't greedy. Once I had £60 in my pocket I'd call it a day and get changed into something a bit more respectable to go out for the evening. If there wasn't a film on that I wanted to see I'd have a meal at a restaurant instead.

That was how I met Spiros. He was a Cypriot, a fat little man with a jet black beard who owned a restaurant where I often used to eat after work.

I'd noticed that above the restaurant Spiros had rooms that he let out to tenants.

He started talking to me one night as I was tucking into my steak. He'd guessed what I did, which wasn't hard, I suppose, even when I didn't have my working gear on, and he asked me if I'd like to rent one of his rooms to do business. God, was I green! All the time I'd been on the game I'd worked for myself, somehow managing to steer clear of all the cons and rackets going on. Stupidly, I thought when he offered me a room that he was doing it out of the kindness of his heart.

One of the reasons I hadn't seen through him was that he was married. He had an Irish wife and they had two beautiful little boys who used to run in and out of the restaurant while she was serving the meals. It didn't occur to me that a family man like that could be a pimp.

So I took the room. I paid him rent and thought that everything was great, but at the end of the first week he came up from the restaurant to see me. I thought he just wanted the next week's rent and I went to my bag to get it, but when I turned round he'd come in and shut the door behind him.

I handed him the rent money, and as he counted it he smiled at me – but it wasn't a friendly smile, like the sort he'd always given me up to now. There was a pause while he tapped the money against his hand and when at last he started to speak he talked very slowly, as though he were speaking to a small child, and a not very bright child at that.

'Now, Gloria, I want the rest of the money. This is not enough.'

'What do you mean?' I asked, indignantly. 'You said that was the amount and I've given it you. What else do you want?'

'My wife has been counting your men for me. You had seventeen clients this week. I take £10 for each of them. That means you give me £170. I think we should be clear about this. Do you understand?'

He stood next to the door, the smile never leaving his lips, his eyes watching my face, while he turned the rent money over in his hands. I think my jaw must have dropped. It wasn't often that I was stuck for something to say, but now it felt as though my tongue wouldn't work.

'You're kidding me,' I blurted out at last, rather desperately. I hadn't noticed before how narrow his eyes were – like a snake's. He tapped the notes against his fingers and grinned.

'Come on Gloria. Hand it over,' he said.

I was suddenly furious as I realized how he'd caught me.

'Get lost!' I bawled at him. 'You never told me nothing about this before. Rent was all you said. I'm not working for anyone else.'

If there was one thing I was sure of it was that. I didn't even like sex. If I was doing it at all I was going to keep every penny. I knew that I'd have to work twice as hard for a pimp and go with twice as many men. I might have been green but I had a good business head on me and I could do my sums. Besides, I liked being my own boss. Why should I work for anyone else?

He didn't say anything when I shouted at him. He just watched me, smiling.

'Get lost,' I said again. 'I'm going. I'm not staying here anyway, so you can forget it. You can keep your flat.'

His eyes turned into slits in his greasy little face. 'You'll be sorry you said that, Gloria,' he said. His voice had gone very quiet.

I shrugged. 'OK then, I'll be sorry. Too bad.'

In my innocence I just thought he meant I'd be sorry I'd missed my big chance to have such a great guy for a manager. But I found out that night exactly what he meant.

I was sitting at the bar of a pub in Shepherd Market, vaguely thinking about looking for a punter, when a hand slipped under my elbow and a voice whispered in my ear: 'Hello, Gloria. You want to come for a walk?'

It was Alkis, another Cypriot I had often seen in the restaurant chatting with Spiros. I didn't like him. One night his girlfriend had argued with him and he had hit her across the face in front of everyone in the restaurant. I looked behind him. The same girlfriend was standing a few feet away now and next to her stood Spiros. All at once I felt as though I were starring in a bad American film.

Alkis' hand moved up my arm and gripped it so tightly that I yelped. Then I found myself being swept through the back exit – part of a happy foursome, as far as anyone watching could tell.

Outside, as they must have known, the corridor led past the toilets to a dark, unlit passageway. Behind me Spiros slammed the back door of the pub shut and leaned back against it as Alkis turned me round to face him in the passageway. Suddenly, without saying a word, Spiros hit me in the stomach. I doubled over in pain and he hit me again on my back. Then while Alkis and the girl watched he carried on landing blows with his fists, holding me up with one hand and punching me in the ribs with the other. At about the fifth or sixth blow I felt a sharp burning pain in my side and I screamed. I thought he'd stabbed me but there was no blood and I couldn't see a knife. Whatever he'd done, he'd done with his fists. He hit me twice more, then stepped back and Alkis pulled me away.

'OK, Gloria, we're all going for a drink and a talk now – all right?' Spiros asked. He was sweating and panting. I didn't answer him. All I could think about was how to breathe: each breath caused the pain to stab through my side again.

They bundled me down a street and into a taxi and we drove to a Greek restaurant in Soho where they seemed to be known to the people who ran it. Spiros hung on to me as I stumbled down the stairs and joked to the guy taking us down that I had had too much to drink.

They sat me down at a table and bought me a whisky. I'd started to get my breath back and the pain had numbed into an ache, but it hurt to breathe deeply and I was still afraid to speak in case I said something to stir things up again. So I just sipped my drink and pretended to read the menu while they talked to each other. I said I didn't want to eat so they ordered for themselves and when they finished eating they got more drinks. Then an Irish guy called Kenny joined them and bought another round, and by the time they'd finished that they were all laughing and patting each other on the back as though they'd just pulled off a big business deal.

Alkis' girlfriend hadn't eaten anything either. She just sat there looking at her nails, smoking and sipping whisky and yawning. She didn't look at me once. I suppose she was there to make it all look normal and innocent. I could have killed her.

Until they'd finished eating and drinking, the men ignored me too, but when at last his belly was full of steak and whisky Spiros leaned back in his chair and looked me up and down. Then he leaned over the table and pinched my cheek.

'Well, Gloria, you're going to work for me now,' he smirked. 'I'm a good boss. You'll find out.'

Kenny, the guy who'd just arrived, leaned back in the chair next to me and put his arm round me.

'Oh? You didn't tell me you were getting a new girl, Spiros. She's not bad. Tell you what, I'll be her first customer. She can come back to my place now. What do you say, Gloria? Want to earn £2?'

He laughed as if he had cracked the joke of the year. They were all gloating over me – they thought they had me trapped. Kenny's hand moved down and started to stroke my leg.

'Come on, Gloria – want to come back with me?' he said again.

I thought quickly and decided to play it as if they had frightened me into agreeing.

'OK,' I said to Spiros, 'you win. I'll work for you. Look, I've got to go to the bathroom first, all right? I've got a stomach ache.' At least I didn't have to lie about that. I stood up and walked quickly away from the table and they let me go – they must have thought Liverpool girls give up easily.

The bathroom was behind the stage. I didn't even go to the loo. I just waited behind the door until a woman came in and as she opened the door I legged it up the stairs and out of the front door. For once there was an empty taxi when I needed it. I jumped in, slammed the door and shouted, 'Take me to the nearest police station.'

But it wasn't like it is in the cinema. The driver turned slowly round to look at me and said, 'You're joking, love.'

'Will you get going?' I screamed. 'Someone's trying to kill me.'

He pulled slowly away from the kerb – but there was no squeal of burning rubber or danger of red traffic lights being jumped. Still, at least we were moving, and I couldn't see any sign of Spiros and his pals through the back window. I breathed a sigh of relief, which made the pain shoot through my ribs again.

'You running this car in then, are you?' I asked the driver. He wasn't amused but he did put his foot down a bit harder.

He took me to a police station – I don't remember which one – and he must have believed my story because he didn't charge me my fare when I got out. I ran inside as if Jack the Ripper were after me.

I don't know what I was thinking would happen next: that Spiros and his slimy friends would be arrested, locked up, given seven years for assault, maybe. But I was in for a disappointment.

I gasped out my story to the two policemen behind the desk. In fact, though I didn't know it at the time, three of my ribs were broken. I pulled up my blouse and showed the police the bruises that were growing purple all down my side.

They weren't interested. One of them, a sergeant, was doing a crossword and looked annoyed about having to stop. I couldn't believe it. They didn't want to know about my beating-up.

'What do you expect us to do, love?' the sergeant said. 'You could have done that yourself with one of your customers getting too rough.'

He was quite nice but firm. 'It's not serious enough.'

'Oh?' I said, indignant. 'I've got to be found dead first before you can do anything. Is that it?'

I grabbed the sergeant's sleeve.

'He says he's going to kill me. Please do something,' I begged him.

It was a lie but I was getting desperate and, anyway, I felt that my being murdered was a distinct possibility after Spiros found I'd scarpered.

The other policeman shook his head and walked away. I could see he was trying not to laugh and that really upset me. The sergeant took my hand off his sleeve as though it were a nasty insect that had just landed on him.

'I'm sorry,' he said again. 'We're very busy. I'm afraid we can't help you. We can't do anything.'

I knew it was time to go. There'd been no point in coming in the first place. Prostitutes didn't have the same rights as other people when it came to being protected by the police. The other girls I worked with had told me they didn't treat you like human beings but I'd never believed them before. Now I knew that somehow I was going to have to go back to my flat, get my things and cope with Spiros on my own. And if I got bumped on the head in the process it would be just too bad. I shrugged.

'OK, thanks for your help,' I said sarcastically, and I turned to go.

'Tell me something,' the sergeant said suddenly – and I turned round, thinking he might be having a change of heart.

All at once his face didn't look so stern, but it wasn't a change of heart that showed on it, just curiosity, and I knew before he opened his mouth what he was going to ask me. The old question: the one half my clients used to ask when they were having a cigarette after they'd been to bed with me. And I was right.

'Why do you do it?' the sergeant said, shaking his head sadly. He leaned forward over his desk.

'How is it that a young girl – a nice girl like you seem to be – ends up in a mess like this? You don't look the type. What's happened to you in your life to make you want to sleep with men for money?' He shook his head again. 'I don't understand it. I don't really.'

I pulled a face, as I always did when people asked me why I did it, and shrugged.

'You wouldn't have time to listen to it all,' I said, and I walked out of the police station with my nose in the air.

But a few days afterwards, when I'd sorted my life out a bit and felt safe again, I started to think about what the sergeant had said about me not being the 'type' and about how he seemed to think that the world was divided into 'nice girls' and prostitutes. I knew a lot of people thought that way. But it wasn't true. After a year on the game I knew that. No girl was ever born a prostitute – there was always a reason, and sometimes a bloody good reason, why it happened.

And I think it was then that I decided that one day, when I had time, I'd try to explain the chain of events that lead to my being half-murdered by a pimp in Soho. Maybe, I thought, it might make people realize that it doesn't always take a special sort of girl to walk the streets, just a special sort of childhood.

2

There are lots of reasons why nice girls turn into prostitutes, but for me I think some of the reasons were already there on the day I was born.

I came into the world at Sefton Park Hospital in Liverpool on 15 April 1951. There was nothing special about me as a baby except that no one knew who my father was, and I think that includes my mother.

Having an illegitimate baby wasn't as common in those days as it is now, but it was fairly common in our house. It was the third time my mother had brought a fatherless bundle home from the maternity hospital to my grandparents' house at 138 Western Avenue, Speke. My sister Joyce was born when my mother was seventeen, in 1933. Six years later she was caught out again with Thelma. Then, twelve years after that, age having made her none the wiser, she came home with me. Later on, when I was six, there was another baby, Christine – the result of one last fling, I suppose – but I never really knew her.

To understand any of what happened to me to make me end up as I did I think you have to understand something about my mother, and as I only knew her for my first eight years, what I know is mostly what I've been told by other people. She was christened Constance Victoria Lovatt, but everyone used to call her Connie, and she was the youngest of my grandparents' six children.

When she was a small baby she had caught meningitis, which in those days killed most of the children that got it. But whatever else my mother might have been, she was always a fighter. Against all of the doctors' predictions she survived, and after eighteen months in hospital she came home to Western Avenue to be nursed. She still needed a lot of care, which can't have been easy for my grandparents with five other children around, but they did their best.

The meningitis had left its mark, though. It had affected Connie's head somehow; she was seven years old before she learned to walk and even when she was able to get about there was always something odd about her. You wouldn't have called her retarded exactly; she could read – though not very well – and add up, and she always knew if she'd been short-changed in the shops, but it was as if, in the way she behaved, she never grew up.

She never developed any sort of sense of responsibility; always seemed to need someone else to tell her what to do; and she had a violent temper which the smallest thing could set off. Later on, with her own babies, she was like a child with dolls, cuddling and playing with them one minute and dropping them and forgetting them when something more interesting cropped up. Maybe it was because the meningitis had damaged her brain or maybe it was being nursed like a baby for all those years that stopped her growing up, or perhaps it was a bit of both. I don't think anyone ever knew.

Whatever the reason, I have to be honest: as a mother, she wasn't too hot – not that she ever literally dropped me, as far as I know, but my sister Joyce says there were lots of times when she'd find me still in my pram in the garden after Mum had gone out for the evening. By the time I was six months old I'd been in hospital twice with pneumonia, even though this was in summer. God knows how I survived my first winter.

As I grew up, Connie spent more and more of her evenings out, and often the days as well. But she hardly ever stayed out all night and when I awoke in the bedroom we shared I would see her big shape curled up under the counterpane of the other bed, unconscious and snoring. Sometimes I'd crawl into bed with her then and snuggle up to her, enjoying the warmth of her body in the knowledge that after a late night out she wouldn't wake up and kick me out.

She never used to come home drunk, though. I don't know where she used to go, but it wasn't to a pub. She was quite strait-laced in many ways and I never saw her touch a drop of alcohol. She said that drink was evil and that people who drank were devils. Another funny thing about her was that she never wore any make-up at all. She used to say that you couldn't improve on nature.

One vice she did have was smoking. I can't picture her without a cigarette between her lips. Joyce told me she used to smoke sixty a day, which must have cost her a fair bit, even in those days. It was odd as she never had much money for food or clothes, even for herself, so I can't believe that she was working on the streets. But looking back now, I think the cigarettes were a clue to where she went and maybe even to who our fathers were. The one place in Liverpool where cigarettes were cheap and plentiful and were used as payment for favours was in the ships on the docks: maybe the nights she spent away were spent on board ships keeping sailors company – which, if it's true, is one of life's little jokes in view of what happened to me later.

In appearance my mother was quite a striking woman – not beautiful, but you'd look at her twice. She was tall, as I am now, about five foot nine, and she had, like my grandfather, a slightly Chinese look about her, with olive skin, and jet black hair which she usually wore loose to her waist but would sometimes pin up in a tight bun on top of her head. I thought it made her look frightening like that; she reminded me of a schoolmarm and I was glad when she took it down again. As she got older she started to put on weight, which was another characteristic I inherited, but because she was so tall it just made her look even more imposing.

I didn't like her very much. I suppose all small children want to respect their parents, to look up to them, to feel they can rely on them. By the time I was five I knew that as far as my mother was concerned I could feel none of this. Although she cooked some of my meals and bought my clothes and bathed me on bath night, she did these things because Nana told her to. For most of the time she was like a lodger in the house rather than a mother, and a lodger who thought children were a bit of a nuisance at that.

Most of the work of looking after me fell to my Nana, Eliza, which didn't please her too much. You could hardly blame her, I suppose. She'd brought up six kids of her own and to tell the truth I don't think she'd liked babies very much even to start with, but in those days there was no pill, so she was lumbered with them. And then Connie turned out to be an invalid, so even when the other five had left home Nana still had her to look after.

Then, to make matters even worse, this invalid daughter had gone out and got herself pregnant and brought two more babies home for Nana to bring up. And fair play, she'd done her duty. I never heard Joyce or Thelma complain about the way they'd been looked after, but it must have been the last straw, when Nana had at last got them grown up and nearly off her hands, for her suddenly to discover that Connie's belly was sticking out again. By that time she must have been well over 70 years old and had just had enough.

The result was that I never got the feeling Nana was particularly fond of me, and that's putting it mildly. In fact she made it obvious I was like a thorn in her side. If I was in the same room as her I seemed to irritate her and nothing I could do was ever right. As soon as I was old enough to think for myself, I learned to keep out of her way. Out of sight was out of mind as far as Nana was concerned, which meant that from the time I could walk I spent more time out of the house than in it. By the time I was five, I was what I suppose you would now call 'street-wise', and would roam miles from home after school – often not coming back until after dark.

I've made it sound as though it was all bad, but there were good things in my life at Western Avenue and one of them was my granddad. I used to call him 'Gang-Gang', which had been my baby name for him, and I loved him more than anyone else I knew. His real name was Benjamin Lovatt. I never knew what his job had been as he had retired long before I was born and used to spend his days sitting in the corner of the kitchen dozing in his armchair. He was a big, kindly, huggable figure and to me he was like my dad, granddad and Father Christmas all rolled into one. If ever someone had made me cry I knew I could climb on his knee and get a cuddle without being asked the reason for my tears or being given a lecture on how bad I'd been.

One of the clearest memories I have of Gang-Gang is of a time when I was about six and I'd persuaded my mum to buy me a pair of roller-skates for Christmas. For some reason – it must have been the fashion then – I had pulled out the new shiny straps and replaced them with long rags. And there was no one I would let tie these skates on but Gang-Gang. I'd wake him up from his afternoon nap and climb on to his knee with my skates. Nana would tell me off for waking him but he'd never grumble and would carefully thread the rags in and out and then stretch them tight and tie them with a bow round my ankle. When he'd finished he'd pull them to test them, then he'd smile at me as though we had a big secret between us and put me back down off his knee. Blissfully happy, I'd skate off out of the back door, ignoring my grandmother's angry cries about the damage I was doing to the kitchen floor.

Gang-Gang used to suffer badly from asthma and every summer he'd go away on a chara for a week at the seaside with a lot of other people who had bad chests. He said the salt air cleaned his lungs out.

On the day he was due back, straight after breakfast, I'd start waiting at the corner of Western Avenue for the chara bringing him home.

Sometimes it would be nearly lunchtime before it arrived, but I wouldn't give up because I knew he'd bring me a stick of rock back. He'd always pretend he hadn't. When the chara at last arrived he'd climb shakily down its steps and look round for me and I'd rush up and hug him.

'Come on, Gang-Gang,' I'd say. 'Give it us. Give it over.'

'I haven't got anything, Gloria,' he'd say, straight-faced.

'Oh – you have! Give it us.' I'd scream with delight and eventually, smiling like a conjuror pulling a rabbit out of a hat, he'd reach in his pocket and hand over a cellophane-wrapped stick of pink rock with 'BLACKPOOL' written right through the middle...

As for the rest of the family, my big sisters were more like aunties to me, being so much older. They were quite different from each other. Joyce the eldest, was eighteen and still at home when I was born, but got married soon afterwards and moved out of my grandparents' home to a house in the next avenue taking Thelma, my other sister, to live with her. Joyce was the brainy one of the family. She'd passed her eleven-plus and had done quite well at school but she was a worrier, Joyce. Unlike me, she was very sensitive about not having a father and for years had told all her friends and even her teachers at school that her father had been killed in the fighting at Dunkirk and she and Thelma were war orphans. I don't think she ever quite forgave me for coming along and spoiling her story, but still she was good to me. I think she felt responsible for me and always used to step in when she thought things were getting out of hand with the way I was growing up.

Thelma, my other sister, was the happy-go-lucky one. I was too young to remember her before she went to live with Joyce but I can picture her when I was growing up as always laughing and going out and enjoying herself. She always looked out for me, though, buying me presents even when it wasn't Christmas or my birthday and taking me with her when she went to her friends' houses. When she was fifteen and I was three years old she was *too* happy-go-lucky one night and got herself pregnant. She had a little boy, Alan, who was taken into care and put in a children's home, because Thelma was so young. But he used to come and visit her at weekends sometimes. Then she'd bring him to see me and we'd go for walks down to the woods.

I used to love going to the woods. Speke in the 'fifties was a great place for kids to grow up. It was quite a well-off area for Liverpool. Though the houses in our road were only terraced council houses they all had well-kept gardens with paved garden paths and clipped privet hedges. An island of grass ran down the middle of the Avenue on which chestnut and cherry trees grew in a neat line and in the spring there was pink blossom everywhere. If you walked past the end of the Avenue down Oglet Lane you were in the country with real farms – and chickens which had wandered out of the farmyard, scratching around in the dust.

At the end of the lane was the wood. Often, after school, and sometimes when I should have been there, I used to find my way to the woods carrying a jam-jar to look for frog-spawn, or dragging big sheets of cardboard to build dens under the trees. Sometimes I'd go with mates from school and in the summer, after we'd spent all day playing soldiers or cowboys in the woods, we'd all come back to our garden where I'd set up a makeshift shower with a hose-pipe and we'd splash about in our cozzies spreading the afternoon's grime more evenly over our bodies.

Once or twice a year the gypsies would camp in the woods on their way to the big horse fair at Appleby. I'd almost live there then, stroking the big black and white horses going round and round on their chains and chatting to the gypsy children and peeping through the caravan windows at all the expensive silver and china laid out inside. Then one day Joyce came looking for me, found me with the gypsies and put a stop to it. She said they'd kidnap me and take me away with them, which I didn't think sounded so bad, but always after that she kept me in her house whenever the gypsies were in the area.

On days when I didn't go to the woods I would sometimes go to Speke Airport. I discovered the airport soon after I started school. I'd see the big planes flying quite low over the playground when they were coming in to land and ask the teachers where they were going to.

The airport was about three miles from our house and it took me more than an hour to walk there. I used to climb up the stairs to the observation floor and watch all the take-offs and landings for a while, imagining I was on board and dreaming about what it must feel like as you watched the earth fall away from you.

Then after a bit I'd go into the departure hall, climb up on a bar-stool and buy myself a milkshake. They cost a shilling – which I'd have conned out of Nana before I set off. I would run upstairs to her bedroom, where she used to lie down every afternoon, and shake her arm.

'Nana, Nana,' I'd whisper. 'Me mam wants a shilling for the meter.' The gas meter used to swallow shillings like chocolates so as long as I didn't get too greedy and make her suspicious, I could always rely on Nana to give me my milkshake money.

I'd spend hours at the airport, watching all the people coming and going, dreaming that I was rich and could fly around the world by plane. I don't think I'd even been in a car more than a couple of times in my life then. Sometimes when their flights were called the people hadn't finished their drinks and would leave their glasses half-full as they hurried off to catch their planes. That was what I was waiting for. I would taste everything they left but soon discovered that the person who'd been drinking before me was the best guide to whether I'd like the taste or not. I learned that fat blonde women in fur coats tended to drink the sweet, sticky sort of mixture I preferred while it was better to steer clear of the glasses left by businessmen in suits, which usually contained stuff that was bitter and nasty.

No one ever asked me what I was doing there, even though I was only six, and no one ever asked me where I'd been when I got home. Half the time my mother didn't really seem to notice if I was there or not. Although she usually helped Nana get my meals and bathed me and put me to bed if she was in, her mind always seemed to be somewhere else and she didn't often speak to me, unless I'd done something to annoy her. But the odd thing about Mum was that although you could say she neglected me in some ways, she'd stick up for me if anyone outside the family had a go at me.

Once, I remember, when I'd just started school, I had a fight with a boy in the garden: one of those kicking and scratching fights that small kids get into because someone has called someone else a rude name. This time things went too far because the boy, who was quite a bit bigger than me, banged my head against the corner wall of the house and I put my teeth through my lip. When Mum saw what had happened she grabbed me, marched me to the boy's house and punched his mother. I remember this seemed to me at the time quite fair, and for a while she went up in my estimation, though I thought she should have punched the boy as well. Then, clucking and tutting and looking really concerned, she took me to the hospital where I had some steel stitches put in my split lip.

Unfortunately for me, once the drama was over she quickly lost interest and instead of taking me home she left me at the end of the Avenue and went off saying she had to meet someone.

I can't have been too upset because I remember that rather than go home I decided to go to the cinema, where a Norman Wisdom film was playing. It was *The Square Peg*, which I hadn't seen before, and it was good – but I had to come out early because every time I laughed it hurt my lip.

I used to love going to the cinema. The nearest one was in Garston, which was even further to walk than the airport but that didn't bother me: nor did the fact that I hadn't any money. At least once a week I used to trot off after school and when I arrived at the Empire I'd stand around begging people to take me in. I must have looked pathetic. I was quite a skinny kid and had a very pale complexion which coupled with my jet black hair always made me look as though I was sickening for something, even though I was pretty healthy. On top of this I was usually dressed in hand-me-downs from my sisters, so the upshot was that someone in the cinema queue almost always took pity on me and paid for me to get in as their good deed for the day.

I didn't mind what I watched, though Norman Wisdom was my favourite – I'd have walked twice as far to see him, but I'd sit through anything I was allowed in to see. Not many people in our street had tellies, so in those days most of the kids in our road used to go to the cinema once or twice a week.

Often when I'd been to the pictures it was after dark when I got back in, but I don't remember ever being frightened on my way home – God knows how I didn't get myself done in, walking through the streets at night at six years old, but someone up there must have been looking out for me.

Then one day my mother told me she was going to have another baby. I don't remember the news making much of an impression on me. I didn't think it had much to do with me. This time the baby was born at home.

I'm not sure if it was meant to be a home birth, or if things just happened too quickly for Mum to get to the hospital. I have a vague memory of Joyce running for the midwife, and then of me sitting in the kitchen with Gang-Gang when Nana came downstairs to say the baby had arrived and it was another girl.

Mum called her Christine. I don't remember much about her except that she was a sickly baby and Mum seemed very wrapped up in her for those first few months, just as though she had a new doll to play with. So she had even less to do with me than before.

That was fine by me. I had got to like the free and easy life I was leading and the less people bothered about where I was the better it suited me. But my days of running wild were numbered and shortly after my seventh birthday two things happened which together led to my life changing overnight.

3

For as long as I could remember my Nana had complained about having pains in her head, and ever since I'd started school she had been lying down each afternoon, sometimes not getting up until it was time to make supper. She seemed to have headaches nearly all the time – and listening to me charging though the house used to make them worse, she said. After the new baby came she started to spend even more time in bed, moaning and groaning. I just thought she was being bad-tempered and miserable. No one ever told me she was ill.

One day I came home late after school to find the house very quiet. It was autumn and already dark by the time I came in, which was not unusual, but what was strange was that there were no lights on anywhere in the house. Gang-Gang wasn't in his chair and there was no sign of my mother. I don't remember feeling frightened exactly – more puzzled, as I couldn't remember the house ever having been empty before. There was no sign of any tea having been made for me, either, which was probably what bothered me the most. I knew that Nana would be upstairs as I couldn't remember her ever going out of the house at all that year and I thought she must have overslept her afternoon nap again.

So with my empty stomach making me brave I decided to risk her anger and wake her up. I went upstairs and turned left across the landing to her room. She hated anyone switching the light on when she was in bed – she said it hurt her head – so I switched the landing light on instead and could just make out her sleeping shape under the covers of her and Gang-Gang's double bed. I crept up and shook her gently by the shoulders. When she didn't move I knew at once that something was wrong. I called at her loudly to wake up but she just lay there. I touched her cheek and it was freezing, like marble, and I started to cry. I knew something awful had happened but I didn't know the name for it. I only knew Nana was gone and I was alone in the dark with something strange and frightening that wasn't her any more.

I think maybe I screamed but I don't recall the next few minutes very clearly. I just remember thinking I had to get away before the same terrible thing that had happened to Nana happened to me. The only thought in my head was to get to my Auntie Dorothy's house, which was in Aigburth. Why in my panic I thought of going there I don't know, because Joyce's house was only in the next street while Aigburth was another part of Liverpool. But, whatever the reason, it was to Aigburth that I half-ran, half-walked, crying and looking over my shoulder as though I thought Nana was going to get up from her bed and chase me.

On the map it's about five miles from Speke to Aigburth and when I finally arrived there I was in such a state I couldn't find Auntie Dorothy's house. I hadn't been there very often, as Auntie Dorothy was one of Mum's sisters who didn't get on with her all that well. I wandered from street to street trying to see a house that I knew until finally I thought I'd found it and rang the door bell. A man I'd never seen before answered the door and said I had the wrong address but at least I was in the right area because he knew who my auntie was.

He said I could wait in his house while he telephoned her – her family were quite well-off and had put a phone in the year before. The man's wife made me lie down when she heard my story and gave me a hot drink and half a crown and by the time my auntie came I had fallen asleep.

I spent that night at Auntie Dorothy's house, sleeping on the couch. She didn't say very much to me except to tell me that Nana had died and gone to Heaven, and after struggling in vain to understand what that meant – I don't think Heaven had ever been mentioned in our family before – I fell quiet myself. I could tell by the way she spoke to me that she felt I was a nuisance and shouldn't have come, and I wished I'd gone to Joyce's instead.

The next morning Auntie Dorothy gave me breakfast and took

me to the bus stop, and after giving me the right fare she turned and walked away without even waiting for my bus to come. Why I should remember that detail now after all these years I don't know, but it must have hurt me that she couldn't be bothered to see me safely on to the bus. It's funny, the things kids notice.

I sat on the bus and tried to work things out. I had seen dead animals before, but this was the first time that anyone I knew had died. I don't think I'd ever thought it might happen to the people around me, although I had seen funeral processions, and coffins covered with flowers. Thinking about that gave me an idea and I knew what I must do. When the bus stopped I ran to the greengrocers on the corner and spent the half crown I had been given the night before on a bunch of yellow flowers for Nana.

I felt terribly guilty. I knew I'd often been bad and rude to Nana and shouted at her when she told me off. Now I wouldn't ever be able to say I was sorry or thank her for all the things she had done for me when my mother couldn't be bothered or wasn't there. I felt the flowers were a way of saying I was sorry.

When I got to our house the undertakers were there and I gave one of them the flowers to take to Nana as he went upstairs. My mother said they were going upstairs to sew Nana up – at least that's what I thought she said, which confused my ideas about death even more. Gang-Gang wasn't there. He must have been at Joyce's. Mum didn't ask where I'd been but I told her anyway and she just said, 'Oh', as though I often slept at Auntie Dorothy's house.

I don't remember the funeral so I suppose I didn't go to it, and to this day I don't know if I was the first person to discover that Nana was dead or if everyone already knew but no one had thought to tell me. Joyce told me years later that she'd died of a brain tumour, which was why she had the headaches and was so bad-tempered all the time.

She also said that Mum's new baby, Christine, was in the room with Nana when she died and must have been there in her cot when I found Nana, though I don't remember seeing her. I don't know if there was any connection but soon afterwards Christine started having fits and went up to live with an auntie and uncle in Scotland to see if a change of air would make her better.

When Nana went the only discipline in my life went with her and soon I was running completely wild. Looking back I'm amazed I wasn't bumped off by some pervert while I was wandering around the streets the way I did that year, and it was soon after this that I came pretty close to it.

It was during the school holidays. If I got fed up with hanging around the house I used to go down to the bottom of the Avenue where all the buses had their terminal at the Pegasus pub. There was a small buffet bar outside the pub, run by a woman called Nora, where the drivers used to get their tea. I kept bothering Nora to let me help her and in the end to keep me quiet she said yes. I used to go inside the buffet and make Oxo drinks and sandwiches for the bus-drivers.

One morning when I arrived at the buffet as usual at about 10 o'clock, there was a strange bloke standing at the side of the buffet, leaning against the wall next to the pub. He had his flies open, exposing himself, and all the time he was looking at me and smiling.

I might have been wild but I was still an innocent as far as men's bodies were concerned. The only man in our house was Gang-Gang and I had never seen him with even his shirt off. So I was looking at this man's penis and thinking, 'What a strange thing!' I couldn't figure out what he was doing and I was frightened and fascinated at the same time. He kept looking at me and smiling as I stood on the buffet steps and I couldn't take my eyes off him. He had a funny, staring look on his face.

'Would you like an ice-cream?' he asked me all of a sudden.

You didn't have to ask me a question like that twice. I said, 'Yes, please', and he held out his hand. It had sixpence in it. I walked up and took it, trying to pretend that I wasn't looking at the fascinating thing he was holding in his other hand. It made me feel slightly sick, the way you do when you pass something that's been run over in the street. No one had ever told me not to speak to strange men, but I felt uneasy and as though I was doing something wrong as I took his money.

I flew into the buffet and asked Nora for a choc ice.

'Oh yes? And where did you get the money for that then – been robbing your mum, have you?' she laughed.

Nora knew that I never had two pennies to rub together but she hadn't seen the man outside. I said nothing.

'Well, you're out of luck, gal. There's no choc ices left. We won't have no more until next Thursday when the van comes round.'

I wandered back outside. The man was still there. He looked at me and said, 'Well?'

'They didn't have none,' I said and handed his sixpence back to him.

He took it and as he did he caught my hand.

'Never mind,' he said. 'We'll get one down the lane. Come on, I'll take you. I'll buy you one down there.' And he started to lead me round the back of the pub towards Oglet Lane.

Now he was talking to a girl who knew Oglet Lane like the back of her hand, and if there was an ice-cream shop down there it was news to me. Open fields, high hedges and murky ditches, yes. Ice-cream shops, no. And yet I went. He let go of my hand and walked ahead and I followed him as if I were on a piece of string. I knew there was something odd about him – dangerous, even – but it was as though I couldn't help myself. I had to do what he asked. He had nearly reached the turning into the lane and I struggled to escape from his spell.

'I've got to go home,' I said, nearly crying. 'Me mam'll kill me. My life won't be worth living...'

But he walked on, looking back over his shoulder and smiling at me, and I kept following him.

There was a large brick wall around the pub making a right-angle into the lane. Once round the corner no one could see you from the buffet or the street. The man stopped at the corner and took my hand again.

'Come on,' he said. 'I'll get you a really big ice-cream...'

Suddenly I heard a door open and a voice screamed, 'Gloria! Get back here before I kill you.'

Good old Nora. 'I'm coming,' I yelled to her. I pulled my hand free and ran back to the buffet so fast my feet hardly touched the ground.

At the same time a bus conductor and his driver, both of them big and black and angry-looking, appeared as if from nowhere and yelled something at the man who'd wanted to give me an ice-cream. He cleared off round the corner and they disappeared after him, yelling all the while.

I didn't understand what had happened and once I was back in the warm buffet I soon stopped being upset and got back to making bacon butties. But Nora was quite pale with shock and kept asking me hadn't my mother ever told me not to go off with strange men; I replied that she hadn't, ever, which was the truth. I didn't know what the fuss was about but I sensed that I had done something wrong...

A few days later the bus conductor and his driver came to the house with a policewoman. She asked me what the man had said and done to me and told Joyce there was going to be a court case (my mother was out when they called and Gang-Gang had to send round for my sister as he had no idea what it was all about). The policewoman said I wouldn't have to go to court as the two men from the buses had seen everything that the man had done and would be able to tell the magistrates everything.

After they'd gone Joyce got quite upset with me for not telling her anything about what had happened. I said I hadn't thought it was that important. Then she told me to go upstairs. As I stood listening at my bedroom door I could hear her talking to Gang-Gang – and then I heard them shouting at each other. I wondered anxiously what I'd done to cause all this trouble. For the next few days Joyce came over to see me every day and I had my meals at her house after school. She seemed very quiet, and every now and again I'd catch her looking at me as if she was about to say something, but she always seemed to change her mind at the last moment and look the other way.

About a week later a man knocked at the door. He said his name was Mr Woolridge and he had come to see me. He was a nice, grey-haired little man who sat down and chatted to me

30

about school and what I did and everything. He said he'd come specially to see me because he'd heard a lot about me, but instead of smelling a rat I was flattered. It felt great to be the centre of attention for once.

Mr Woolridge asked me if I would like to go on holiday. I said, 'Great! Fantastic!' I'd never had a holiday but I knew all about them from Gang-Gang's stories of his chara trips. I knew they happened at the seaside with donkeys and sand and Blackpool Tower and best of all Blackpool rock. It was all arranged there and then, and the date was fixed for my departure. Mum was home that day and she asked if she should buy me some new clothes, but Mr Woolridge said not to bother.

I couldn't believe it. Having been fairly unpleasant since Nana had died, my life suddenly looked rosy. I remember Gang-Gang seemed unhappy and worried about something but I thought he was just upset that he would miss me during the week I was away.

I gave him a big hug and told him that this time it was my turn to bring a stick of rock back for him. He still looked sad, but it never occurred to me that Mr Woolridge hadn't said when I'd be back. I thought all holidays were for a week. If they'd told me then my 'holiday' was going to last more than eight years they'd have had to drag me screaming out of the house.

Meanwhile, my mother ignored what Mr Woolridge had said and took me shopping in town for new clothes. I was thrilled, though when I saw what she'd bought me I wasn't so pleased. I can picture my new outfit even now if I shut my eyes: a white silky blouse, a green tartan skirt with white mohair stripes running though it, black brogue shoes and white socks. I wasn't very grateful. I thought her taste in clothes was terrible.

Everything happened quickly after that and a few days later I was at Joyce's house, dressed up in my new outfit, waiting for the kind people to come and take me on holiday. I was over the moon when they arrived – not in a chara, as I'd expected, but in a car. My mother wasn't there but Gang-Gang had come to say goodbye. He was crying; big fat tears rolled down his face as he held me close to him. I was touched. I knew how much I loved him but this was the first time he'd shown that he felt the same way about me.

'Don't worry, Gang-Gang,' I said as he dabbed at his eyes with his hankie, 'I'll be back soon. I'll bring you a stick of rock back.' (That's what he always used to say to me. I felt very grown-up.)

Then I walked off with these two women, both of them grinning like Cheshire cats and holding my hands tightly, one on each side, as though I might be thinking of running away. I said goodbye to Thelma and Joyce, but when I turned to wave to Gang-Gang he was going back inside the house, his face buried in his hankie. Years later that still upsets me whenever I think of it. I never said goodbye to Gang-Gang. And I never saw him again.

4

I sat in the back of the car as we left Liverpool and the two women sat together in the front talking to each other in posh voices. I could hardly understand them. I felt left out and unimportant again. Now and then they turned round and asked me polite questions about how old I was and where I went to school, and when I answered them my accent sounded strange and common – even to me.

I slumped down in the back seat, holding the bag which contained my pyjamas and clean knickers close to me, and looked out of the window as the city streets changed to fields. I wondered what the sea would look like and whether I would get to go up Blackpool Tower.

But the sea never appeared. Instead we went through the Mersey tunnel to Birkenhead and started following the bank of the Mersey back through Port Sunlight and Bromborough. My sense of geography was not that bad and by the time we reached the outskirts of Chester I had twigged that we weren't on our way to Blackpool. I asked the women where we were going but all they did was to smile as though they had a wonderful secret and to say that we would soon be there.

At last the car slowed down and turned up a long tree-lined drive. The woman in the passenger seat turned round and reached for my hand. I hid it under my pyjama bag feeling in the pit of my stomach that something was wrong.

'Here we are, Gloria. This is where you'll be living,' she said, smiling. 'This is your new home.' If she thought she was breaking it to me gently she was mistaken. My mind wouldn't let me accept what they were telling me. I told myself that they just meant my holiday home. But it wasn't what I had been expecting and I was taken aback by what I saw. In front of us as we came out of the trees stood what looked like a haunted house from one of the horror movies I sometimes sneaked in to watch at Garston. Spooky – that was the only word for it: a huge mansion with dark windows and an enormous brass-riveted front door. It was three-and-a-half centuries old, I later found out, so it had had plenty of time to build up an atmosphere. To a kid coming from a terraced house it looked terrifying.

The women walked me up the steps to the front door, each holding one of my hands again, with the lady who'd driven the car carrying my bag. The other one, who was still wearing a big, false smile, lifted up the huge door knocker and let it fall. After we'd waited for ages, footsteps sounded, running downstairs inside the house, and the door was swung open by another smiling lady. She was aged about 40, with grey hair set to look like corrugated iron. She said hello to the women as if they were long-lost friends, then looked down at me.

'And you must be Gloria,' she said.

I nodded silently.

'My name is Miss Jones, but everyone here calls me Auntie so I hope you will too.' She pronounced it 'arntie' instead of 'antie', as I was used to. I'd never heard such posh accents before. Even the teachers at school had had Liverpool accents. I felt as though I was in a foreign country.

We went inside and 'Arntie' took us into a huge sitting room. She brought the women a cup of tea and I had a glass of squash and a biscuit, and then the women who had brought me stood up and said they must be going.

'Goodbye, Gloria,' they said, and patted me on the head and left. They'd done their bit – their charity work was over for the week – and I was left alone with my new auntie.

She smiled at me and asked if I'd had anything to eat. I had trouble understanding her and she had to repeat her question. When the penny dropped I said no, I hadn't eaten. It was about 2 o'clock in the afternoon but I'd been too excited that morning even for breakfast.

'Come along then,' she said, and led the way out of the lounge, shutting the door behind her. It was the only time I remember having been in that room in all the years I was there.

I followed Auntie into a huge kitchen. She reached into one of the range of ovens along the wall and pulled out a plate of food. 'We've been keeping this hot for you,' she said, smiling. From being ravenous my stomach suddenly turned over. I still remember that first meal: liver, carrot, turnip and boiled potatoes. The whole day was going wrong. I hated and loathed liver. I was hungry for chip butties and scouse.

She sat me at a little table in the kitchen and left me to eat. I tried the liver and choked. Everything seemed to stick in my throat. After five minutes I gave up and scraped it all off the plate into a bin under the sink. Auntie returned ten minutes later and took my plate away. She came back, still smiling, and asked if I would like to meet some of the other children I was going to be living with. I said all right, not at all sure that I wanted to, and she led me down a corridor into a playroom full of little children, all younger than me. I suppose the older ones must have been at school.

As soon as they saw us the kids all ran up to Auntie and stared at me. I felt like a zoo animal. No one said a word, but they all formed a circle around me and stood sniffing and looking up at me, as though I were some exhibit Auntie had brought to show them.

I flapped my hands at them. 'Go away,' I said crossly. I didn't want snotty-nosed kids crowding round me. Auntie stepped in quickly. 'Now, Gloria, that's not nice,' she said. 'If you're going to live here with us then you must learn to be friendly to the other children.'

I spun round in horror to face her. 'What?' I said. 'I'm not living here. I've come on holiday for a week. I've promised my granddad I'm going home.'

Auntie didn't seem to know what to say. In the end she just smiled and shook her head.

'We'll talk about that tomorrow, Gloria. Why don't you come into the next room? We've got more toys in there. Maybe you'll find something you'd like to play with. I have to go and do some work now but I'll come back and see how you're getting on later.'

I followed her unhappily through another door to a playroom where a rocking-horse and a sand table stood. There were pictures on the walls and pretty curtains and, best of all, a bookcase full of adventure books and annuals. I loved reading. I cheered up. Maybe my holiday wasn't going to be too bad after all.

It was then that I saw Alan, Thelma's little boy. He was standing at a table rolling a ball of plasticine and he smiled shyly at me, his big eyes looking sad – as they always did.

'Hello, Auntie Gloria,' he said.

That was the moment when the penny finally dropped and I realized where I was ... and that I was trapped. Alan lived in a children's home and there'd been no mention of *him* coming on my holiday with me. This must be where he lived.

'Hello, Alan,' I said. I was close to tears. I'd been well and truly conned and I knew it. I went over to help Alan with his model-making, furious with everyone but most of all furious with my mother, who I was now sure had arranged this whole thing. She'd never bothered about me all my life and this was her way of telling me I had become too much trouble now she had the new baby. I hated her and I spent the next hour taking it out on the plasticine. If I'd had any pins they'd have been sticking in a fat little model of her.

Later that day another member of staff came on duty. She was known as Matron and was the second-in-command at the home, her boss being Miss Jones, or Auntie, who was the superintendent. Matron was a small woman who, I found out later, suffered from rheumatoid arthritis, but she wasn't exactly a frail little old lady. Alan told me that she had a terrible temper and I started to find out about it on my first night.

None of the other kids, apart from Alan, spoke to me that afternoon, probably because of the look on my face as I murdered the plasticine, and I ignored them all in return. When the older kids came in from school they started poking fun at my Liverpool accent, so I swore at them in the worst language I knew, which I don't think was too bad but which seemed to impress them enough to make them leave me alone.

Tea, which I picked at, was at 5 o'clock. I couldn't eat. I felt deserted, alone and betrayed. I couldn't remember ever being so unhappy. At 7 o'clock Auntie told me it was bedtime, and although I had never been to bed that early in my life I was pleased to go.

The final insult of the day came when Auntie led me into the nursery. A bed had been made up for me in the corner next to the cots. Auntie said the girls' bedroom was full so I would have to sleep with the babies for a few nights. I was too miserable to protest.

That first night was horrible. Matron was on the prowl. She was on night duty, which meant that she sat on the landing listening for disturbances. I don't know how long she sat there. It can't have been all night but it seemed to me to be in the middle of the night when I woke up with a start. This wasn't unusual for me since Nana died. Ever since the night I'd found her body three months before, I'd been having nightmares about her coming back to haunt me. I used to dream she had come back to life and was chasing me with her head all sewn up as my mother had told me.

Now when I woke in the nursery it was after one of these dreams. A cool breeze was blowing on my face. The bedroom window was open and in the dark I could just make out the curtain blowing out in the draught like a ghost. After everything that had happened that day it was too much for me and I let out a howl of terror and started to cry. Of course, the baby in the next cot heard me and joined in and soon the whole nursery was screaming and yelling in sympathy.

Suddenly the door was flung open. Matron stood in the doorway, her shape outlined in the light from the hall, and her voice hissed across the room, 'Gloria! Be quiet! Stop it!'

But I couldn't stop. Now that I'd started crying it was as though my body had a will of its own and however much I tried to hold it in my sobs kept going. All I wanted was an arm round my shoulders – a kind voice telling me it was a bad dream. But I didn't get it. Instead, something hard hit me between the shoulder blades and I stopped crying with the shock of it, only to wail even louder as I realized what was happening.

When I'd got undressed I'd put my new brogue shoes neatly side by side under the bed. Now, as she came over to me, Matron picked up one of these shoes and began hitting me with it. I couldn't believe it. I'd never been beaten in my life before. I started to scream as if I were being murdered and Matron's voice grew louder to match my screams. She told me I was being selfish; I should think of others; I was keeping the whole home awake. She couldn't bear spoilt children, she said. And each time she stopped for breath she aimed a fresh blow at my head, my shoulders or my back. I buried my face in the pillow and covered my head with my hands, and at last, as the feathers muffled my sobs, the blows slowed down.

When she was satisfied that I wasn't going to start again Matron made a big show of going round all the cots and tucking in the crying babies. Then she came back to my bed and stopped. I froze, but all she did was to toss my shoe back under my bed before turning the light out and disappearing out of the door. So that was my first lesson and I learned it well. I never cried out loud in the night again.

The next morning I was moved from the nursery into the girls' bedroom, so my outburst did at least get me away from the babies. After moving my things, I was sent downstairs to start learning the routine of the place.

There were 26 children living at the home, although the number varied a bit as some of them went home for weekends. Our days started at 7 a.m., when Matron came into the bedroom and switched the lights on. We had to turn back our beds to air them and get washed and dressed for 7.30, when we had breakfast in the main dining room. Auntie and Matron sat together at a separate table and there were five oblong tables for the children. Breakfast was usually cornflakes or porridge followed by scrambled eggs and bread and butter or by bacon which they used to cook in the oven, so it was all soft and greasy. They never seemed to use a frying-pan, whereas at home almost everything we ate was fried so the food tasted different. For a long time I hardly finished a meal at the home.

I remember the fat bacon was what I hated most. Each rasher used to consist of tiny slivers of meat surrounded by masses of fat. We were supposed to eat it all and not trim any off. I'd always hated fat and I used to cut it all off and hide it under my bread, then, when the others were finished, I'd leap up to volunteer to stack the plates and neatly slid mine with all its fat trimmings into the middle of the pile. Matron caught me doing it once and made me eat all the trimmings on their own but I only pretended to swallow them and spat them out down the toilet as soon as I got out.

I hadn't been at the home very long before I realized that my life there was going to be a battle with authority. I'd been doing what I pleased for too long to take kindly to obeying orders, and right from the start I was always in hot water for being disobedient.

Most of the trouble happened with Matron. Auntie was all right. She used to talk to you and reason with you when you misbehaved. The children at the home quite liked Auntie. Unlike Matron she seemed to be fond of children, but even so she had 26 of them to look after so she wasn't always there when you wanted to talk about a problem. There were often a lot of unhappy children at the home and it was asking too much for one person to try to give love to them all, but Auntie did her best.

Matron was different. When you misbehaved she'd lose her temper before you even said anything to defend yourself. She was very strict and she hardly ever smiled. 'Boot Camp' we called the place when Matron was in charge. We all used to feel she hated us and we certainly hated her.

Because there were so many disturbed children at the home Matron and Auntie often had to deal with what they called 'behaviour problems'. The most common of these was bed-wetting. They had developed their own strange 'cure' for this, which didn't come from any textbook, and it wasn't long before I sampled it at first hand.

Soon after I arrived, and while I was still having nightmares about Nana haunting me, I woke in the early morning to feel a strange warm sensation spreading around my back and legs and I realized with horror that I had wet my bed. I was so ashamed; it had never happened to me before. I was also terrified. I already knew what the punishment was for this crime. I tried desperately to disguise what I had done by pulling the sheets back and making my bed before breakfast instead of leaving it to air as we were supposed to do, but Matron was wise to this trick. I was discovered and the bed-wetters' cure was doled out to me.

First I had to strip the bed and wash the sheets and hang them out in the garden to dry. Then I was taken to the bathroom and given a cold bath by Auntie – and I mean *cold*. I don't think she meant to be unkind. She really thought it would work. But knowing her reasons didn't stop me screaming as she held me down in the cold water.

Whether this treatment had been passed down by previous Matrons and Aunties from Victorian times or whether it was all their own invention I don't know. What I do know is that it certainly wasn't a miracle cure. I wet the bed every night that week, which sometimes meant that I was washing the sheets at 5 o'clock in the morning as once I'd woken up I couldn't bear to lie in a wet bed.

Every morning I was given the cold bath treatment, too, and once, when I hadn't woken in time to wash the sheets, they were dumped in the bath with me. On Saturday morning I woke when Matron came in only to discover I had done it again. I got uncomfortably out of the bed and had just started to pull the sheets back when Matron came up and saw what had happened.

'Don't bother getting dressed, Gloria,' she said. 'You're not getting up today. Get those sheets washed. Then you can get back to bed.'

I spent the whole of Saturday in bed in disgrace – and every

Saturday after that if I'd wet my bed during the week. Perhaps in the end the treatment really did work, or maybe I would have grown out of it anyway, but after about three Saturdays in bed I woke up one morning to find a miracle had happened and the sheets were dry. After that my 'accidents' got further and further apart until at last they stopped completely. But I never got over the worry of thinking it might happen again and I was so terrified of Auntie's cold baths that for years after that I never used to drink anything after tea at 5 o'clock; so instead of waking with wet sheets I used to wake with a dry throat, gasping for a drink of water.

There were six girls in our bedroom. It was quite a pretty room with curtains and pictures, and outside you could see the trees, which was nice in the daytime but creepy when you woke in the middle of the night. We kept our clothes in a locker and over a chair beside the bed. Bedtime stayed at 7 o'clock for the first two years I was there and after Matron put the lights out no talking was allowed.

Before bedtime each child in the home had a job to do, and this would change by rota each week. Cleaning the shoes was the one that everyone hated the most. There were 26 pairs of them. One child would put the polish on and another would brush it off. By the time you were finished you'd be black and need a bath.

Another two children had to do the washing-up each week, while two more laid and cleared the dining-tables and so on. They had staff there to help with the work as well, of course. There were usually two cooks and two part-time cleaners on duty, but the cleaners seemed to spend all their time cleaning the floors: not surprising, really, with our 26 pairs of feet skating round them. Because of this everyone old enough to help had to do something to help keep the home tidy, and when you finished the job your work would be inspected to see if it was up to scratch. Everyone over ten years old had to wash their own school clothes in the sink at night as well – blouse, pants and socks – and then hang them up so they'd dry while you were wearing the other set the next day.

The home supplied our clothes – most of them were donated to the home by well-wishers and had usually been worn by someone else first, but sometimes people would give us rolls of material and then Auntie would sit down and sew for a week and for a while afterwards we would all be dressed in red paisley or mustard flannel – it was usually some awful design that people hadn't been able to sell in their shops.

To a kid coming from my background the whole atmosphere and routine of the home made it seem like the army. There were set times for everything, set duties, set rules and set clothes to wear. It was probably very good for me, having spent my life until then not knowing the meaning of the word discipline, but it was nasty-tasting medicine and I hated almost all of it.

One completely new experience for me was going to church. Every Sunday morning we would walk down to the parish church in a ragged crocodile and sit crammed into three pews which seemed to be kept specially for us. No one else ever sat in them, anyway: maybe they thought they'd catch something. Nearly always I fell asleep during the sermon, but it was my loss because after Sunday lunch Auntie would ask us questions about what the vicar had said and if we got it wrong we wouldn't get any dessert. So naturally I missed out most of the time.

In my first six months at the home I didn't see any of my family at all. They didn't write to me or visit me but I told myself maybe they hadn't been allowed to. It never occurred to me to write to them. People didn't write letters in my family. I don't think I'd ever written to anyone in my life.

Then one day Auntie called me into her office and said she'd had a letter from Joyce to say my grandfather had died – just like that. By the time they let me know about it he was already buried. I didn't say anything to Auntie but I locked myself in the toilet and cried. No one ever knew how much Gang-Gang meant to me and after he died I stopped wanting to go back to Western Avenue and started to think of the institution as home.

It was another year before my mother came to see me, and when Matron came into the playroom to say Connie was there I

42

ran upstairs and said I didn't want to see her. I still thought that she was the one who had 'put me away', and so, to my mind, it was her fault I was living in this place I hated so much, and also, in some confused way, I felt it was her fault that I'd never see Gang-Gang again.

They brought me downstairs and took me into Auntie's office to see her, but I wouldn't speak to her. She asked me a few questions and I just looked at the floor. After a bit she gave up and went home. She came once more to see me a year later, but I wouldn't answer her when she spoke to me on that occasion either. She never came again.

5

Every cloud has a silver lining, and there were certain perks to living in a children's home which I gradually discovered during the first few months I was there.

One of these perks was that there were always lots of people who wanted to take us children out to Sunday tea. Quite often these people were rich, and as far as I was concerned they were the best sort. I got a visitor quite soon. Her name was Miss Jacobs. She had a nice Bentley and she'd been all over the world – Hawaii, Africa, India – and she'd tell me all about it while I listened with my mouth open.

She didn't pick me: I picked her. I remember there was a meeting in the church hall. I think it was the British Lions Club who arranged it so that people who wanted to meet children could look them over and make up their minds which colour, sex and age they fancied while we were supposed not to know what was going on.

Of course we all *did* know, and guessing that no one would pick me out for my looks I quickly decided not to wait and made a bee-line for Miss Jacobs. She was sitting in a corner on her own, not saying anything, but I noticed all the jewellery she had on – lots of diamonds around her neck (at any rate they looked like diamonds to me) – and I started talking to her before anyone else could grab her. She must have been about 50 years old, I suppose, but she was great. She told me about all these places she had been to and then she asked if I'd like to come to tea with her. I pretended to be surprised and said yes.

She used to come to the home on a Sunday afternoon and pick me up in her Bentley. She seemed to like me and would take me out quite often. Matron said she couldn't understand it, but I felt it was a feather in my cap. Even at my age I knew it meant status to have a Bentley and all the other kids used to crowd to the door to see it when it arrived.

I blush now when I think of what Miss Jacobs must have thought when I first started visiting her. My table manners were terrible. Funnily enough I'd been taught quite good table manners by Nana, but it was since being in the home that they'd gone downhill. So when Miss Jacobs said, 'Help yourself' at the tea-table, I'd dive in as though I hadn't eaten for a week. It was like being at a banquet. She had this great long dining-table and we'd sit, one at each end, facing each other while we ate. I'd help myself to food from her sideboard, which was always laden with goodies when I came to visit.

Her food was lovely. There'd be boiled ham and salad – in the home it was always Spam – and then for dessert there'd be peaches with fresh cream or a gâteau. I used to go mad and stuff my face full of cream chocolate cake. When I couldn't eat any more we'd go into what she called her drawing room, which was full of beautiful furniture and antique china and paintings, and she'd play lovely music at the piano and tell me tales of foreign lands and as soon as my tea had gone down a bit I'd have some chocolates.

When it was time to go she'd give me ten shillings and some toffees to go back with and I'd drive home with her in her Bentley in a blissful dream. Then I'd make all the other kids jealous with tales of what I'd done and eaten and said.

It gave me back some self-respect, having Miss Jacobs. If someone like that could like me I felt I couldn't be as bad as Matron made out, and I used to live for Sundays when she came. I think she visited me for about three years until she moved away. Each Christmas she'd meet me in town as a special treat. I remember her taking me to Marks and Spencer and buying me a brown corduroy skirt and a nice blue sweater, and afterwards she took me to Quaintways, which was a lovely little tea-room in Chester. I don't remember what we had for dinner but I remember having Arctic roll for dessert and guzzling so much of it I felt sick.

It was Miss Jacobs who noticed when I was nine that I was having trouble with my eyes. I used to leaf through her books on foreign countries and she said one day, 'Gloria, why are you holding that book so close?'

When we got back to the home she went in to see Auntie and told her she thought my eyes needed testing. They made me an appointment and, sure enough, the test showed that I was badly short-sighted. I was given brown-rimmed National Health specs with thick lenses which made my reading a lot easier, although they didn't do much for my appearance.

So I had a lot to thank Miss Jacobs for. But although I was grateful for her friendship, I always had the feeling I wanted more than a friend who took me out once a week. I felt that I was a small part in a lot of people's lives but there was no one to whom I was really important. I think that's all anyone wants, really – to be really important to one person. I knew that I used to be important to Gang-Gang, but since he died there was a terrible gap in my life that no one seemed able to fill. I used to tell myself that Joyce cared for me – and I think she did in her way, but she was busy with her husband and her own babies who had started to arrive. I used to imagine that Joyce had won the pools and would come and take me away to live with her, but as time passed and she didn't come to visit me at the home I found it harder and harder to believe in my fantasy.

Until we were old enough to take the eleven-plus all the children at the home went to the local primary school, which I didn't mind. I wasn't exactly a star pupil but the one subject I did like was English, and I read my way through the school library while I was there.

The most important thing about school to me was that it was where I met my friend Susan. She lived quite near the home and I thought she was wonderful. We hit it off right from the start. She was a big girl and very sporty, even at primary school. Later on at secondary modern she turned into a javelin star. Her mother used to feed her as though she were building her up for a weight-lifting competition, which explained her size. Her mother's teas were great: sausage, egg and chips, followed by cream cakes and anything else you wanted, and of course I used to have these too when I went round to her house after school.

I hadn't known Susan long when I discovered she was in the Salvation Army. She asked me why I didn't join. Straight away I realized that this was a way of avoiding going to church with Auntie and all the other kids, having to answer stupid questions on the sermon and missing my dessert.

So one evening after school I asked Auntie if I could change my religion to the Salvation Army. She wanted to know why and I said that I was interested in playing the instruments, which I wasn't at all, but she believed it and to my amazement they bought me all the kit – the red tie, the blue skirt and the jacket – and I went along. One thing they did encourage at the home was any sign of your turning religious.

After I joined, I started getting taken out to tea by all the brigadiers and their wives. Their teas weren't as good as Miss Jacobs' but they were OK; from that point of view the Army happened at just the right time because Miss Jacobs was moving away from the area and I knew my Sunday outings with her were soon going to stop. I soon realized I was on to a good thing at the Salvation Army. Not only did I become a regular attender, but when Susan joined the band so did I. It was only shaking the tambourine but it was good fun.

There were always plenty of Army events to go to as well, which got me out of the home. One day, I remember, there was a sort of fête, and it was opened by the Duchess of Westminster. I couldn't take my eyes off her. She was very well dressed and she was wearing an enormous ring with a great big stone in it. I made up my mind to get to know her.

I was helping on a stall when she came past and I started talking to her – about how I liked her clothes, I think. She was really nice and chatty. She asked where I lived and I told her I was in a children's home – I knew by now that this was a guaranteed way of getting people to feel sorry for you. Sure enough, at the end of the fête when I was trying to decide how to get back (Auntie had already left), the Duchess of Westminster came over and asked if she could give me a lift.

Her car was a Rolls-Royce, which she drove herself instead of having a chauffeur. When I asked her why, she said it was because she liked driving and didn't see why she should pay someone else to do something she liked doing herself. I sat in the front next to her and stared out at the people walking by, watching them turn to look at us as we glided down the road. I wondered if they were trying to guess who I was and I tried to look superior and important.

The Duchess chatted away about all sorts of things and I leaned back on the leather seat and dreamed that she was my chauffeur and I was the Duchess of Westminster. I just had one wish left and I couldn't think of a polite way to make it come true, so in the end I just asked her, 'Do you think I could try your ring on?' She laughed, then took it off her finger and passed it to me. I slipped the diamond over my knuckle and imagined I was rich. I decided I would like it.

When we got to the home she said I must go to have tea with her at Eaton Hall. She kept her word. A couple of weeks later her car came for me and took me to her massive stately home for tea. I wasn't that easy to impress, though. I remember being really disappointed because instead of the pheasant and smoked salmon I'd imagined rich people ate for tea we just had a big plate of cucumber sandwiches.

You didn't go out a lot from the home unless you joined something like the Salvation Army as I had done. In fact, we were rather isolated most of the time, and apart from going to school some of the children hardly left the home at all in the winter months.

In summer, though, in the school holidays, we used to go on day trips to the coast, so at last I achieved my ambition of getting to the seaside. Someone – British Rail, I think – gave us free tickets and we'd go to North Wales for a few hours on the beach at Colwyn Bay. That was great. Once when I was nine we went for a week to Rhyl, where we stayed in a big hut and slept in sleeping bags on the floor. Another time we went to Llandudno and I got lost on the Great Orme, nearly causing a search party to be sent out. I loved the seaside. Even Matron didn't seem so bad when we were on holiday.

Not everyone at the home was like me – a long-term inmate. Some of the children were just there for a short while because their mother was in hospital or because their parents had marriage problems, and when things got better they'd go back to their real homes again; so the kids were always changing.

One girl I remember in particular was called Elizabeth. She was really beautiful but she always looked sad and frightened. Her mother had got divorced and wasn't able to look after her. But about a year after she came to the home her mother got married again and her new father came and took her on holiday with them to Switzerland. When she came back, it was with the news that he was going to adopt her as his own daughter and she was going to leave the home and live with him and her mother. We were really happy for her. It was nice in the home in that way. There wasn't much jealousy. I think you just felt pleased when something good happened for someone else because it made you believe that maybe, one day, it could happen for you.

The whole time I was at the home I could never manage to stay out of trouble for long. When I was about ten I discovered cigarettes. I used to go to Susan's house every Thursday and we'd have a ciggy on the bus going to tambourine practice and another on the bus coming back and then we'd have some spearmint chewing gum to take the smell off our breath before we got off. I used to get my pocket money – half a crown – every Saturday, and I remember going into town every Saturday morning and buying five Park Drives. I'd smoke two or three on the walls at Chester and take the rest home.

But it was always a problem knowing where to hide them. One Saturday I went down to the games room and hid my Park Drive packet in the top of the piano; then I shut the lid and went outside to play with the other children. Just my luck – it had to choose that day to rain. Matron clapped her hands together and called us all to her in her bossy headmistress's voice.

'Come on, children. Downstairs to the games room.'

My stomach started to turn over and, of course, as I'd feared, once we got down there she decided to entertain us on the piano. It soon dawned on her that several of the notes sounded funny.

'That's odd,' she said, swivelling around on her piano stool and looking straight at me. 'This piano was only tuned last week.' And with that she lifted the lid and pulled out my Park Drives.

There was none of that silly nonsense of innocent-until-proved-guilty for Matron.

'Gloria, I want to see you in my office,' she said.

'Me, Matron? Why, Matron?' I asked, putting on my best wide-eyed look.

'The office, Gloria.'

That was it – no questions, no defence, just the ruler right across the knuckles. This was the standard punishment. Sometimes she would hit you across the face with the ruler, too, if she was in that sort of mood, but today I was in luck. It didn't stop me smoking but from then on I found better hiding-places.

Matron's habit of going mad with the ruler was the cause of my losing one of my few friends at the home. Maria was a secretary who only worked there during the day. She was foreign – Swiss, I think – and she was so sweet and pretty and softly spoken that she reminded me of the fairy godmother in *Cinderella*. I would go and see her every day in her office and take her sweets or a flower. I used to suck up to her something rotten. It wasn't the first time I had latched on to a member of staff. I was becoming known for it.

I used to be a real pain to new staff. I was so anxious to make them like me that I would come on too strong and follow them round talking nineteen to the dozen. It had the opposite result to what I wanted and put most of them off, so they used to avoid me and turn and walk the other way when they saw me coming. But not Maria. She seemed to understand that all I was looking for was attention, and she gave it to me.

If I had had an ideal of the sort of woman I would like to have been when I grew up, then it was her. I don't know whether she knew how much I hero-worshipped her, but one day she took me for dinner with her family and it was every bit as good as I expected it to be.

Her family were just like she was, quiet and smiling, and – it's hard to explain – they just gave you the impression that they all loved each other. There were no raised voices, they didn't criticize each other, and the parents didn't say, 'Stop doing this' or 'Why don't you do that?' to the children. It was beautiful – a warm, loving, relaxed family, and for a time I was a part of it. I forgot all the pain of being away from my own family, and the home seemed a long way off.

I remember having a little wine with my dinner and wondering whether Matron would smell it on my breath – and, if so, what she would do to a child who not only smoked but drank as well – but Maria just laughed and said she would never know if I didn't tell her.

Afterwards we went to a farm and then for a walk in a park with some of Maria's brothers and sisters. The last thing she did was to give me a box of Rose's chocolates before she took me back to the home in time for bed. It was the first time I'd ever seen what a normal, happy family life could be and it made a big impression. That day is as clear to me now, more than 25 years later, as if it were yesterday.

You get a feeling of being cut off from real life when you're in an institution. Even if the staff are really good it's not the same as being in a family, so most of us used to grab every chance we had of getting involved with a real family. That was why my best friend was Susan rather than someone else in the home. We were all the same in the home. It wasn't that we didn't like each other; we just preferred to make friends with children from outside to give us a chance of seeing how proper families lived.

The main trouble with being part of a big 'family' of 26 children was that it set you apart and made you feel different. You weren't just a child. You were a child from a home. You found yourself doing everything together. You'd go to church, go to Brownies or Guides, go on holiday, all in a group, and you'd get cut off and start feeling different from other children unless you were careful.

So my friendship with Maria and her family was very important to me. But it didn't last very long. Soon after my visit to her home Maria left, after having a big argument with Matron over me.

The row started because Matron had hit me across the face with her ruler one day when I'd been cheeky. Maria had stood up to her and told her she shouldn't do that. The next thing I knew, Maria came to me in tears to say she was leaving the home. She didn't tell me why she was going but from the way Matron had been shouting at her I suppose she was sacked.

I was eleven and I remember I had just started at secondary modern school, which I hated, when Maria left. I was miserable for weeks after she'd gone. That was another of the troubles with being in a home. You couldn't pretend people were like your family, even if they were nice, because they went away. It had started with Miss Jacobs, who had moved to live somewhere else just when I felt she had become a good friend. Now it was happening with Maria. No one ever seemed to stay more than a couple of years at the home, so just when you thought you'd found someone who was like a big sister or an auntie to you they went off to another place to look after some other children. It was just a job to them.

It was more than a job to Maria, though. I knew that, but still I couldn't help feeling that a person who really cared about me would have stayed and stood up to Matron. At eleven years old I didn't understand that she probably had no choice.

Not long after Maria left I got shingles quite badly and was so ill I had to stay off school for nearly three months. I hadn't told anyone I had a rash and it just got worse and worse until one day Auntie found me bent double over one of the radiators in the corridor trying not to cry because the pain was so bad from all the scabs round my middle.

I was taken to the doctor straight away. After he'd examined me he asked if I was worrying about anything. He told Auntie that shingles in someone my age was often due to nerves. I said I wasn't worrying. There didn't seem any point in telling him about Maria now she'd gone but I still think her leaving could have had something to do with my being ill.

I had to stay in bed for over a month after that and the doctor said I was to take it easy and do nothing strenuous for another six months, which at least meant I got out of shoe-cleaning.

It was that same year that Matron announced she was retiring and leaving the home. We didn't exactly break our hearts over it. I don't think anyone had thought of Matron as a big sister. But soon afterwards Auntie said she was going too – I think she was taking up another job somewhere else – and I was sorry about her. She was the one who used to supply the love and affection, while Matron doled out the discipline. You always knew that if you had a problem you could go to Auntie with it and she would try to help. I don't think she knew how bad Matron could be when she lost her temper because I'm sure she wouldn't have allowed it.

But although everyone felt a bit sad about Auntie I don't think we really grieved over either of them. We were too excited at the thought of getting new superintendents and wondering what they would be like. We built up rosy pictures in our minds of how they would look and speak and treat us.

I hadn't heard the saying then 'Better the devil you know', but in the years to come I learned what it meant. Six months after Matron and Auntie left the home most of us were wondering why we'd ever complained about anything while they were in charge. If we'd known what was going to replace them, we'd have kept our mouths shut.

6

Uncle John, his children and his wife Sandra, together known as the English family, arrived with the furniture van one morning in February just before I was twelve.

Uncle John was quite a fat man – in his forties, I suppose, not very tall, with glasses. He had a shiny complexion as though he were sweating all the time, but the most noticeable thing about him was his limp. He had suffered from polio at some time in his life and as a result he hobbled rather than walked and he wore a special built-up shoe on his bad leg which soon caused us to nickname him – brilliantly, we thought – Uncle Peg-leg.

His wife, Auntie Sandra, was very much in his shadow. Where he was fat, she was skinny, with blonde hair and a permanently worried expression. She told us her job around the home was going to be supervising the cleaning and cooking and looking after the girls, while it seemed Uncle John was to be the big chief, responsible for discipline and decision-making.

Our new superintendents had three children of their own – two boys, fat like their father, and a little girl – and they were brought in to meet us. The little girl was only a toddler and quite sweet, but we took an instant dislike to the boys. They looked smug and superior and when they said hello it was as if they were royalty talking to peasants. I suppose we were bound to dislike them whatever they were like for having what we hadn't got – a family – and for having it right in front of our noses, so maybe we didn't give them much of a chance; but before their first week was over they got the message about what we thought of them and after that they stayed in their part of the house and we didn't see them much.

But we hardly had time to notice whether the boys were there or not, for we were too busy getting used to the ways of our new superintendent. Uncle John dominated our lives at the home from the word go. We had thought of Matron as strict, but Uncle John obviously felt that he had to show us who was boss right at the start if he was going to control us properly.

The first night after the Englishes moved in Auntie Sandra took Matron's old place in the chair outside the girls' bedrooms to make sure we went to sleep. Bedtime in our dormitory was 8 o'clock now, after which no talking or reading was allowed. Naturally we were excited by the day's happenings and there was a lot of whispering and giggling which didn't go down too well with Auntie Sandra. She must have complained to Uncle John because the next night he took over from her and sat listening outside the door. We were no better that night – after a day at school we couldn't just switch our minds off at 8 o'clock and we'd been whispering about boys and clothes and the new family for quite a bit when Uncle John burst in and switched the light on.

'All right, girls,' he said very loudly, and we all froze. 'Out of bed. Line up at the door.'

Puzzled, we obeyed, and he led us down the corridor in a long line. One of the girls asked if she could put her dressing-gown and slippers on but he said no.

At the back part of the house the corridors were tiled with those big red quarry tiles and he led us along them shivering in our brushed nylon nighties. It was a frosty night and there was no heating in the back of the house. At the end of the corridor he stopped and looked angrily at the six of us.

'I'll make you tired enough to sleep,' he said.

Then, one at a time, he led us to different doorways in the corridor and made us stand in front of them. We were scattered all over the back of the house, not one of us near enough to talk to the next one, all barefoot on the cold tiles. Then he went off to the kitchen to have supper with the other staff. He left the kitchen door open to make sure we didn't shout to each other and we could hear them all laughing and talking from where we stood. He didn't come back for nearly an hour, by which time we were all frozen, our teeth were chattering, and the two smallest ones, who were only seven, were crying. That night I decided I hated Uncle Peg-leg, and it was the start of a war of wills which lasted until I left.

The punishment didn't stop us talking, of course. From then on Uncle John instead of Auntie Sandra always sat outside the girls' dorm listening to us and the night-time trips down the corridor became a regular part of our lives. Sometimes he'd change the way he punished us. A few times he made us come down and polish the dining-room floor on our hands and knees in our nighties. After an hour of that we *all* hated him.

Uncle John thought up other original treatments for wrongdoers over those first few months. If anyone misbehaved during the day he would lock them in the broom cupboard on the landing, sometimes for just ten minutes but often for a couple of hours. It was pitch dark in there and there was a strong smell of polish and disinfectant which I hated more than the dark. With my objection to discipline I used to spend quite a lot of time in the broom cupboard and I soon worked out that I could make life more comfortable for myself if I thought ahead. One evening when Uncle John was out I sneaked up to the landing and hid a torch and two books – Rudyard Kipling's *Jungle Book* and *Just So Stories* on a shelf behind the dusters. After that whenever I was locked in for answering back or being untidy or some other major sin I would dig them out and settle down to a good read while Uncle John thought I was repenting of my wicked ways. By the time I came to leave the home I must have been the country's greatest expert on big cats and jungle life.

But it wasn't just the discipline that was bad. It was the complete lack of any affection towards the children. We realized now just what we had lost when Auntie went, because although she could be strict she never lost her temper and at least when the little ones cried she would put her arm round them, and often she would pick the babies up out of their cots just because she felt like giving them a cuddle. All of that stopped when the Englishes took over as superintendents.

I was the oldest in our dormitory by now and I sometimes felt as though I had to be a mother to some of the others myself. We had two little 7-year-old black girls in with us whose parents had split up and didn't want them. They used to wander around holding each other's hands and looking as though they hadn't a clue where they were. I felt so sorry for them. Maybe I identified with them because of what had happened to me. I could see that all they wanted was some attention, but no one ever seemed to notice they were there. I don't remember Uncle John or Auntie Sandra ever speaking to them except to tell them to hurry up or get dressed. They never made any effort to get to know them or find out why they looked so sad.

There were often black babies in the nursery, too; I used to walk around with them nursing them as though they were dolls, but apart from that, after the Englishes came, they were only picked up to be fed and changed. I never saw anyone cuddling them or playing with them the way you should with babies.

There was a little toddler called Shirley who I think was West Indian and who had been in care since she was one. She was always crying and she used to walk around with a dirty, runny nose all the time. I used to wipe it for her but if I didn't it was just left to run. Uncle John used to smack her and push her away if she came crying up to him.

'Shut up. Stop whining,' he'd say. And yet his own little girl couldn't do anything wrong. He was always picking her up in front of us and cuddling her and we all saw the difference.

One of the little boys was called Billy. He was about eight years old, a sweet little kid, who always seemed to be ill and who cried very easily. You only had to say 'Boo' to him. He had a visitor like my Miss Jacobs, a man called Mr Dutton who used to take him to his home every Sunday. One day Mr Dutton asked Uncle John if he could buy Billy a puppy for Christmas. Uncle John said no, the children weren't allowed pets. But a month later, when Christmas came, lo and behold what did Uncle John buy his own little boy as a Christmas present? A puppy. It really upset Billy. He came crying to me on Christmas morning and said, 'Why is he allowed to have one and I'm not?' He couldn't understand it.

What made it worse was that the Englishes also had favourites among the children staying at the home. If we'd all been treated the same way it wouldn't have been quite so bad, but they changed the rules according to whom they were dealing with. There was a family of Chinese children who had arrived soon after me. They were really beautiful, with pale faces and huge dark eyes. One of them, a little girl called Susan, was one of their special favourites and never seemed to get into trouble when the rest of us did.

There was a British girl too, called Mona, who was really pretty. Auntie Sandra took a special liking to her and used to take her on shopping trips to town and visits to the cinema with her own children. All the rest of us who weren't favourites resented it, and used to call Mona names when Auntie Sandra wasn't around to look after her.

But the thing which upset me most about Mona was her hair. They let her grow it long and it was really lovely, blonde and wavy. She used to wear it plaited for school but when she came home she would wear it loose around her shoulders so it made her look like a princess. I was madly jealous and I begged Auntie Sandra to let me grow mine long too, but she wouldn't; as soon as it reached below my ears she used to chop it off, as though I were a boy. I couldn't forgive her for that. With my thick glasses and tall, gangly body I was already self-conscious about my appearance. I was a real ugly duckling and as far as I could see I was growing up into an ugly duck. I used to imagine that if only I could grow my hair long I'd be beautiful like Mona, and that, as I could see, brought its own rewards.

But for every favourite the Englishes had another child they used to pick on. One of them was Alan, my sister Thelma's little boy. He was a bit slow at school but if anyone shouted at him it made him worse. He couldn't think straight then. One day we were all having our tea and Alan came home late from school. Uncle John was sitting at the table and asked him where he'd been. Alan was very timid and he'd stammer and cry if anyone frightened him and he began to stutter now.

'Come on, spit it out,' said Uncle John, and at last Alan managed to blurt out that he'd had to do some extra work after school.

At that Uncle John started making fun of him, saying how stupid he must be to need extra work. Alan just stood there with tears running down his face and his cheeks going bright red as all the other kids started giggling, glad it wasn't them that were being made fun of.

I couldn't stand it. I threw my chair back and shouted at Uncle John, 'Leave him alone. Pick on your own kids.'

That did it. I got a backhander across the face and he started shouting at me. He said Alan and I were as bad as each other and the reason was that our family was no good and we were no good either and unless we changed the way we behaved we never would be any good. We'd end up just like our families – bad, and in trouble with the police.

That wasn't fair. None of my family was in trouble with the police that I knew of, but I knew better than to say anything. When he'd finished insulting me I was sent up to my bedroom without being allowed to finish my tea, but I didn't regret it. I hated the way he bullied the little ones. I knew kids had to be told off sometimes, but he should have taken them away from the other kids to do it. Pulling Alan to pieces, making him cry in front of all the others, making a fool of him – that wasn't going to help him: it would only make him worse. Even I knew that, and I was only a kid myself, not a so-called expert in child care as Uncle John was meant to be. I felt sure that I'd done the right thing but I knew it was going to mean a lot of trouble. And it did. Uncle John had it in for me after that night.

My next big brush with him was partly my own fault, I suppose, and came after the first and only time I ever stole anything in my life. When I was twelve I went home for the first time to Liverpool for Christmas. The Englishes didn't want me to go. Auntie Sandra told me, as Uncle John had, that my family was no good and that they were a bad influence on me. She said that I was better than they were now and if I went back to

Liverpool it could undo all the good the home had done for me in the past five years. For once, though, they couldn't stop me. I had made up my mind to go.

Two days before Christmas Joyce came for me in a friend's car and I travelled back to Liverpool with them. I stayed at Joyce's house. I told her I didn't want to see my mother and the message must have got back to her because she kept away. By this time Joyce had quite a few children of her own, and I'd kept all the toys I'd been given since I got to the home so I could give them to her kids.

Four years at the home listening to Auntie's accent had turned me into a posh kid by Liverpool standards. I remember Joyce taking me to the chip shop and I saw these three little girls sitting in the chip-shop window with their socks round their ankles and all their knickers showing and I said, 'Don't they look common!' in a superior sort of way that had Joyce in hysterics – though I couldn't see what she was laughing at.

It was lovely over Christmas. Everyone was giving presents to each other and kissing, and when I brought out my toys everyone kissed me. It made me feel great.

When I got back to the home loaded with presents from my family I had an idea. I was so full of peace and goodwill to mankind that I thought I'd try and make a fresh start with the staff. Auntie Sandra had always been all right with me so I decided to give her a Christmas present.

I ran upstairs to the store-room where all the spare linen for the home was kept and in the back of one of the drawers, as I already knew, they had some lacy handkerchiefs in boxes. I took a box out, wrapped it up in some of the paper from my own presents and took it to Auntie Sandra.

'Here you are,' I said holding it out to her. 'I've got you a Christmas present.'

She opened it, looking stunned. 'Gloria, how nice! Where did you get them?'

I shrugged. 'Oh, this antique shop in Liverpool,' I said.

'You bought them? For me? Oh thank you, Gloria.' For a

terrible moment I thought she was going to cry. 'That's really very, very nice of you,' she said smiling, and put her hand on to my shoulder – which was the first time she'd touched me the whole time I'd been there. I mentally congratulated myself on my brilliant idea.

Three days later Auntie Sandra called me into the office. Uncle John was there. He was pacing up and down. He looked at me as though I had crawled out from under a stone and then, slowly, from behind his back, he pulled out the box of handkerchiefs. My heart felt as though it had stopped.

'Gloria' (his eyes bored into me but he managed to smile at the same time), 'where did you get these from?'

I knew it was hopeless but I stuck to what I'd told Auntie Sandra.

'Oh, there was this antique shop at home in Liverpool …' I began.

He interrupted me before I got any further. 'That's a cock-and-bull story and you know it.'

I said nothing but watched in horror as he turned the box over and held it up in front of me. There, stamped on the bottom, were the words 'Property of …' and the name of the home.

There wasn't a lot I could say.

I don't remember the punishment that time but I do know that after that I was marked out as a thief. Whenever anything went missing in the home it was assumed that Gloria had taken it. Or at any rate I was the main suspect. It was my own fault, I suppose. Apart from those handkerchiefs I never stole anything at all, but from then on you couldn't tell Uncle John that. Once, a couple of cigarettes and some money were stolen from one of the nurses who worked at the home and I was punished for it, although I'd sworn blind I didn't do it. Then, much later, they discovered that all the time it was a boy called Edward who had stolen them.

By the time the Englishes had been there six months I was branded as a troublemaker and I found myself missing Maria more than ever. She had been someone I could go to when I felt life was unfair. Now there was no one. But someone up there must have been watching out for me because just after Christmas a new helper called Auntie Angela joined the staff.

Since Uncle John came to the home the staff had been changing all the time. Maybe other people found him difficult to work for, I don't know, but it made life hard for the children: you'd only just got to know someone when they were replaced by someone else. By this time I had got a complex about meeting new people. I became convinced that no one could like me and knew that Uncle John told them all to watch me because I was a thief. So I didn't pay much attention to Auntie Angela at first when she came except to notice jealously that like everyone else she spent a lot of time talking to pretty, popular Mona.

Then one day I was in the dorm when Auntie Angela came in and came over to me. 'How would you like to come to a gymkhana with me, Gloria?' she asked.

I was suspicious. I didn't trust anyone by now.

'What are you asking me for?' I said rudely. 'Why should I want to go? Go and ask Mona.'

She didn't take offence. Instead she sat down on my bed.

'I'm asking you, Gloria, because I know you like animals and I thought you'd enjoy seeing a gymkhana.'

I was curious in spite of myself.

'How do you know I like animals?' I asked.

'Because you're always reading animal books,' she said, pointing to a pile of them beside the bed.

I felt a glow inside me. It's people noticing things like that about you that makes you feel special. I decided Auntie Angela wasn't so bad after all.

She was right. I did enjoy the gymkhana. We had a great time and she took me out every Saturday after that. We became good friends. She was the only one of the staff who made me feel I was all right and not bad as Uncle John said I was.

But any good Auntie Angela was doing for my self-respect was soon to be undone completely.

I was twelve-and-a-half now and at secondary modern school,

which meant I was always quite late getting back to the home in the evening because I had to catch two buses. One night I was later than usual because I'd been playing rounders. All the other kids had finished their tea and were downstairs in the TV room. I came in through the back door – Uncle John didn't allow us to use the front entrance – and went to the kitchen. We weren't supposed to be in the kitchen without a member of staff to supervise us, but I was starving. All I could find were some biscuits so I took a couple and went up to the dorm.

It had been a hot day and after the rounders I was feeling sticky so I decided to have a bath instead of watching television with the others. We had our own bathroom which opened off the dorm. I started to get undressed and put my blouse on the chair ready to wash it after my bath. As I laid it down a door opened and closed downstairs and I heard the shuffling noise that meant Uncle Peg-leg was on the prowl. I'd eaten the biscuits so I didn't worry about it and carried on undressing.

We never used to close the dorm door during the day and I didn't now. I took my pants off, then went through to the bathroom and ran the water. I'd just stepped in when I heard the dorm door close and then heavy footsteps coming towards the bathroom door. I called out, 'Uncle John?'

His voice came back from the other side of the bathroom door. 'What are you doing, Gloria?'

'I'm in the bath. I've been playing rounders,' I said, wondering what I'd done wrong this time. 'What's the problem?'

'No problem,' he answered. 'I want to talk to you.'

'OK, I'll come downstairs when I get out,' I said, wishing he'd go away.

'No, don't be silly. I'll come in and talk to you now. I've got children of my own,' he said, and he pushed the bathroom door open and came in, shutting it behind him.

I was sitting down in the bath and I covered my chest with the flannel as he came in. There wasn't much of it to cover. I had only just started to develop. I felt frightened but I couldn't have explained why.

'Where's Auntie Sandra?' I asked.

'She's busy with the children,' he said, looking at me. 'Come on, stand up. Don't be silly. I'm not going to hurt you.' He took me by the elbow and lifted me to my feet.

'Now, get out of the bath,' he ordered. I obeyed him. There was nothing else I could do.

'I'm worried about your schoolwork,' he said. His free hand started playing with my breasts. I tried backing away but his hand gripped me tighter. Then his hand left my breasts, moved down and undid his trousers.

I didn't know what he was doing. No one had told me anything about the birds and the bees. I thought he was going to kill me, but he didn't. Instead he laid me down on the bathroom floor and in a way I wouldn't recommend to anyone I was introduced to sex.

Afterwards he stood up and fastened his trousers back together. His face was red and he was panting.

'Don't you dare tell anyone about this or you'll be in trouble,' he warned me.

I shook my head. I couldn't speak.

'No one will believe you anyway if you tell them because you come from a bad family. You know that, don't you?'

I must have nodded and he looked satisfied. 'Good – just remember that. Now get back in the bath.' And with that he left me.

I sat on the wet lino shivering. I was bleeding. Slowly I stood up and got into the bath. It was going cold. I picked up a nailbrush and kept washing myself, scrubbing myself to get clean. It was all I could think of to do.

I must have sat there for half an hour going over and over what had happened in my mind. I didn't cry. I couldn't. I felt numb. I couldn't understand what he'd done or why he'd done it. I only knew he'd hurt me in a new and horrible way. I thought about telling Auntie Angela but I knew I never would. I didn't even know the words to talk about what he'd done to me and I didn't want anyone to know about it. I felt dirty and ashamed as though somehow what had happened had been my own fault.

After a long time I got out of the bath and put my nightdress on. I decided that night to run away.

7

I wasn't brave enough to run away on my own and it took a week for me to persuade anyone to come with me. In the end Mona, Uncle John's favourite, said she'd come. I didn't tell her the truth about why I wanted to go. I just said I was homesick and because her family lived in Liverpool too she said she'd join me.

We planned to go one night after school. We were supposed to be going to Girl Guides that night, but we hid our shorts and T-shirts in the bushes down the drive and changed out of our Guide uniforms as soon as we were out of sight of the house. Then we took two bikes from the sheds and set off. I didn't know how far it was to Liverpool or how long it would take us to cycle there. I hadn't thought it out at all. I just had a vague idea that if only I could get to Joyce everything would be all right. I wasn't really thinking straight. Every time I'd seen Uncle John in the past week I had gone hot and cold all over. All I knew was that I had to get away.

But the whole thing was doomed from the start. We hadn't got very far before we discovered that both bikes had slow punctures. On top of that, neither of them had working lights or brakes – but we pedalled on down the main road anyway, looking for signs to Liverpool. We had scrumped some apples from the orchard behind the home to keep us going on our way. After a bit it got dark and we left the main road because of having no lights. We were pedalling down a lane when a police car passed. What with us bouncing up and down in our saddles because of the punctures and the bikes showing no lights I suppose it wasn't surprising that the police stopped us. They took us to the police station, soon worked out where we were from and phoned the home. We'd hardly been away more than three hours and Auntie Sandra had only just missed us.

The police were quite nice to us. We were hungry by now and when the desk sergeant took out some sandwiches and started to eat them my mouth watered.

'Swap you a sarnie for one of my apples,' I said hopefully.

He laughed and passed a sandwich over. I shared it with Mona. I was learning that a little bit of cheek could get you a long way. It crossed my mind for a moment to tell him about Uncle John, but as soon as I thought about it I knew it was a stupid idea. If he didn't believe me and told Uncle John what I'd said I'd be in even worse trouble. In any case I wasn't even sure that what he'd done was against the law.

Then Auntie Sandra came. She was terribly polite to the sergeant and kept apologizing for all the trouble 'her girls' had caused him, but she didn't say a word to us the whole way home and I knew we were in for it; or rather, *I* was in for it.

I was right. When we got back, Mona was sent to bed and I was taken into the office to face the Englishes on my own. I couldn't bring myself to look Uncle John in the face, but for once he didn't say too much. He left it to Auntie Sandra, who didn't need any help. She went on and on about how ungrateful I was after all that the home had done for me and what worry and trouble I'd caused everyone by my thoughtlessness. She said my worst crime had been to lead Mona astray. She knew that Mona would never have thought of doing something so dreadful on her own and I was obviously a bad influence on her.

I stood looking at the lino and pretending to listen to her. I wondered what she would say if she knew what her husband had done the week before.

When she had finished lecturing me Uncle John said my pocket money would be docked for a month as punishment. Then I was allowed to go up to bed.

I wasn't put off by our failure. I started planning the next escape straight away. It took me a couple of months to organize but in spite of that it was no more successful than the first one. The trouble was that all the other kids had heard that I had tried to run away and half of them decided they would like to come with me the next time. So when the great day came for my second attempt it was more like a mass break-out than the undercover operation I had planned. In the end there were six of us – all colours, yellow, black and white. I decided we wouldn't go by the main road this time, but would go up-country instead, into the mountains. God knows where I was hoping to get to. I don't think any of us truly expected to get away with it – it was a gesture, that's all – but the whole thing was hell.

We went on foot this time, because there weren't enough bikes to go round. My memories of the police on the last occasion meant that every time we heard a car coming I shouted at everyone to dive for cover, but on my third trip into the bushes I landed in a bed of nettles and was stung from head to foot.

By the time it was dark we were already wishing he had never started out. We decided to spend the night in a new housing estate which was being built outside a village we passed through. After creeping into one of the houses which hadn't any doors in yet we lay down on the rough concrete floor and tried to sleep.

My planning really wasn't too hot. We didn't have any sleeping bags or blankets and although it was only autumn it was freezing. We left at 3 or 4 o'clock in the morning after finally realizing we weren't going to sleep a wink and set off miserably up the lane to the next village. We were trudging up what felt like the side of a mountain when two cars with blue lights stopped in front of us and once again I found myself being bundled into a police car. I think we were quite glad to see them really...

It was the same story all over again. In Uncle John's eyes I was obviously the ringleader so I took the punishment. It was 6 a.m. when we got back to the home. The other girls were sent upstairs to bed, just as Mona had been, and I was kept down in the hallway. This time Auntie Sandra left the lecturing to Uncle John. He waited till the others had gone, then came towards me.

'I suppose you think you're smart, do you, Gloria?' he asked.

I knew what was coming. Where Matron had used a ruler Uncle John used to swing his hand and he smacked me with it now right across the face. Then he gave me a repeat performance of Auntie Sandra's speech about being ungrateful and finally I was put to stand in the passage until it was breakfast time while the others slept it off.

I had to do the washing-up for a month. I didn't really mind being punished. I hadn't expected to be let off but I really resented being the only one to carry the can. I might have been the brains behind it but the others weren't sheep. They had minds of their own. But they got off scot-free. I wished now I hadn't given in to them and had gone on my own. Maybe I'd have got back to Liverpool if I had.

But I didn't really believe it. I was beginning to feel that I was trapped at the home for ever. I had no power – no control over what happened to me. I knew that now. The only people who had any power were the grown-ups and they would use it just as they liked.

I decided that morning, leaning against the passage wall rubbing my nettle stings, that I wouldn't try to run away again. There was no point. Instead I would have to make the best of a bad job. If I had to live in the same house as Uncle John for the next three years then I would find ways of spending as much time away from the home as I could. I would find other interests, other things to think about. I would fill my head with things that would force him into the background and I would keep out of his way and avoid him as far as possible, so that that night in the bathroom could never happen again. That was the best I could do.

I had never been much good at keeping resolutions but I kept that one. From that day on I threw myself into school activities like someone who'd been converted to a new religion.

Since the age of eleven I had been catching two buses every morning to get me to Hoole secondary modern school. I had taken my eleven-plus but no one, including me, had been surprised when I failed it. Until then I had looked on school as a complete waste of time, and although I was an enthusiastic reader my taste was for adventure stories and animal tales rather than school books.

My first year at the secondary modern school had been interrupted when I caught shingles. I'd fallen behind in my work and was put back into the D-stream – the Dumbos. I hated it. The teachers treated you as though you were funny in the head, and I think some of the kids were. The work was so simple a 5-year-old could have done it, and the result was that I played around. I think I was what they call a disruptive influence.

At the end of my second year, after all the happenings at the home and my decision to get involved, I suddenly started to work. Over the next twelve months the difference was noticed because in the summer after I was fourteen my teacher asked the headmaster to move me up and the following term I found myself in 4C. It was great: the work was more interesting and I used to tuck myself away in a corner of the television room when I got home from school and do my homework like a real swot while the other kids watched children's TV. It would have been easier to work in the quiet room at the back of the house but I never did anything on my own now if I could avoid it. I never even took a bath any more unless the other girls were in the dorm. The memory of that night wouldn't fade however hard I tried to push it away.

At the end of my first term in 4C I came top. Straight away I was moved up again, and the next term, in 4B, I came second. After that, the following year I was promoted to 5A and suddenly people were talking about O-levels.

There was one teacher at school who paid special attention to me, Miss Bellis. Funnily enough she was also the first teacher to stick me in detention. She was quite strict but she was kind as well. She would come to the home at Christmas to see me, bringing me Quality Street chocolates. She knew I liked animals and used to buy me books about big cats. I was still crazy about lions – so much so that I decided I wanted to work in a circus or a zoo when I left school. I didn't need to keep my books in the broom cupboard now because since I had started keeping out of Uncle John's way I hardly spent any time in there. It was almost as if he were avoiding me as well, I saw so little of him. So I read the books at night under the bedclothes and learned all about tigers and jaguars and leopards.

I tried to join in as many out-of-school activities as I could. Once, to my delight, I was allowed to go for a week in the Lake District with my class from school. We stayed at a place called Newlands and went boating, walking and rock-climbing. We climbed Green Gable, Great Gable, Great Scarfell Pike and Cap Bells. I loved it – but for one thing: Auntie Sandra had refused to let me take a dress. She insisted that as we were rock-climbing, all we would need were jeans. Of course, when we got there we found that there were dances nearly every night and I was left a wallflower in blue denims while my classmates twisted away in their best frocks, which their mothers had kindly thought to pack for them.

Being a wallflower didn't really matter to me as I wasn't too keen on boys. My views of men in general were a bit dim by now. Even so, having a boyfriend meant status in our group so I was quite pleased for that reason when a boy called Melvyn decided I could be his girlfriend. It wasn't exactly the love affair of the century. It had started with him having to kiss a girl as a forfeit when we were messing about one break at school.

When he chose me, I couldn't believe it, but he told me later that the reason he picked me was that I was the only girl in the group at the time who didn't have a cold sore on her mouth. Even so, it was the first time a boy had kissed me and so from then on in the eyes of everyone else in the form we were a couple. It didn't last very long. I didn't actually like kissing and I don't think Melvyn did much either, so after a few weeks we 'finished' with each other with no big regrets.

I was a late developer physically and at the age of fourteen I still hadn't started my periods. It didn't bother me because I didn't know anything about periods. I was the oldest girl in our dormitory so none of the others had started and whether it was because she forgot or was too embarrassed I don't know, but Auntie Sandra hadn't told me anything, or given me any pads, or prepared me in any way for what was to happen.

It seems strange to me now that I hadn't talked about 'the

curse' with the girls in my form, but I was a bit of a loner at school and apart from Susan I didn't get involved in heart-to-heart talks with anyone.

The result was that I was thrown into total panic one day when I went to the toilet after lunch and discovered a brownish stain on my pants. My first thought was that I had messed myself, and my second thought was that since I hadn't even known that I was doing it I must have something wrong with me – maybe I'd got some terrible disease. Maybe I had a tumour in the head like Nana...

I went to the school secretary crying my eyes out. She was a nurse as well as a secretary and she was the person you went to when you got sick at school. She asked me what was wrong and I told her that I'd dirtied my pants and I'd be murdered when I got home.

She took me to the sick-bay and found me some clean pants to put on. Then she looked at my dirty pants and started laughing, which really upset me.

'Gloria, you're having a period,' she said.

I looked at her blankly.

'Hasn't anyone told you about periods?' she asked disbelievingly. I shook my head.

So then the school secretary explained what was happening inside my body and how babies were made and everything else. It was the first official piece of sex education I'd ever had and I listened open-mouthed.

When she'd answered all my questions she gave me a pad to wear and by the time I got home Auntie Sandra had had a phone call to tell her what had happened and she'd put some more pads in my drawer, though she still couldn't bring herself to talk about it to me. She never mentioned it. Uncle John did, though. That night at tea he sidled up to me and leered, 'I hear you're growing up, Gloria,' he said.

I blushed furiously and ran out of the kitchen. He made me feel dirty and confused. I had understood most of what the school secretary had told me and while the talk had solved a lot of puzzles that had been worrying me it had created another one. I knew now that Uncle John had been trying to make me have a baby that night but I couldn't understand why – or why doing it had hurt me so much. I knew I had a lot more still to learn about sex.

All the time I was at Hoole secondary modern school my closest friend was still Susan Parry. I was allowed to go to her house for half an hour after school and sometimes I could stay for tea, which helped stretch out my time away from the home.

In our third year Susan started throwing the javelin. I quickly realized that here was something else which could give me an excuse to go home late so I took up the javelin too and got pretty good at it, though not as good as Susan, who always managed to throw that little bit further than me. I think it was because I got fed up with always being second in the javelin that I decided to try throwing the discus.

It turned out to be a lucky choice. I don't know if it was because I was the right shape or size but I soon decided that this was the event for me. At the age of fourteen I could throw 103 feet and I was one of the stars of the school team.

I really fell in love with athletics. Part of the reason, still, was the time it gave me away from the home. As well as after-school practice, there were lots of away matches at other schools and sometimes I could spend whole Saturdays at school sports meetings. But on top of that I found that I really enjoyed competing and winning – especially winning. It used to give me a terrific thrill to improve on my previous best throw or to throw further than someone who was older or bigger than me. It did my ego the world of good to discover at last that I had a real talent for something. And then it all came to an end overnight...

One day – it was the middle of October and quite cold, I remember – I stayed behind after school and practised the discus with the gym teacher. I did this quite often, trying to improve my technique, and Susan sometimes stayed too. This night I was the last one to go. I kept throwing better and better and I got carried away because I knew if I kept going I could break my personal best and on my final throw I did just that.

It was 4.45 when I packed up, on top of the world because the gym teacher had said if I kept improving at this rate I could be selected to represent the county the next year. By the time I got back to the home it was 6.30 and I'd missed tea. There was no one about when I got in. I knew Uncle John and Auntie Sandra would be in the front living room and with a bit of luck hadn't heard me come in. I crept into the kitchen and made myself a hot cup of Ovaltine as quietly as I could. It was strictly against the rules but I hadn't eaten since lunchtime and I was starving.

I'd just poured the drink into a cup when Uncle Peg-leg walked into the kitchen.

'What do you think you're doing, Gloria?' he asked, although it was perfectly obvious to anyone what I was doing. I felt my heart start to pound.

'I've been practising, Uncle John. I threw a hundred and three feet...' I began.

He wasn't interested. 'I'm asking what you're doing now,' he repeated, spitting out the words.

'I'm making myself a drink because I missed tea,' I answered.

'You know the rules,' he said angrily. 'You must ask before you do anything in the kitchen.'

'Yes, but it was 6.30 and everyone had left,' I protested. 'There was no one around for me to ask permission.'

'Don't argue with me,' he said through his teeth. 'You've broken the rules. You're always breaking the rules.'

I decided to try an apology as a last resort.

'I know, Uncle John. I'm sorry, Uncle John.'

'*Sorry*, Gloria? Sorry is a bit too late.' And with that he took the drink from me, walked over to the sink and poured it away.

All my simmering hate for him boiled up inside me.

'You bastard,' I said.

He turned round slowly, not trusting his hearing.

'What did you say?' he asked disbelievingly.

'Why did you waste the drink?' I said, still angry but beginning to be frightened. 'It was made with milk.'

'What did you just call me?' he repeated slowly.

There was no point in denying it.

'I called you a bastard,' I said in a whisper.

His face twisted up as he stepped towards me and I knew I was in for it. But even though I had seen Uncle John angry before I wasn't prepared for what happened next.

Something seemed to snap inside him and he started to hit me as though I were a punch-bag. I fell to the floor trying to protect myself and rolled up into a ball. He gave up using his fists and began kicking me: he had special shoes on with steel tips and they felt like bricks hitting me in the side. I tried to roll away from him. I was terrified. I was sure he was going to kill me. After all, he had a good reason. I was the only one who knew what he'd done to me that night in the bathroom and now he was going to make sure I never told anyone about it.

I rolled underneath the table but still he kept on kicking me and all the time he was bawling, 'I'll show you, I'll show you,' and the saliva was spitting out of his mouth everywhere. I was crying and sobbing, 'Don't! Don't!' and at last he stopped and stood panting over the table. It took a while before he had enough breath to speak again, but when he did he spoke in a low, shaking voice and said, 'Don't you ever say that to me again.'

I cowered behind the table leg and after a while he turned and hobbled out of the kitchen. I waited until I heard the living-room door shut before I crawled out from my hiding-place and stood up carefully. My body hurt all over. I couldn't stand up straight and I half-walked, half-crawled up the stairs to the bedroom and crept under the covers of my bed.

When the other kids came up no one said anything, though they must have heard the row in the kitchen. It was 'look after yourself' there now. It didn't pay to ask too many questions.

The next day I was covered in purple bruises from head to foot and it must have been obvious to the Englishes that questions would be asked if I turned up at school looking like that, so I was kept off school for a week. When I got back I found out that Uncle John had sent a note to my teacher saying I'd fallen downstairs. I don't know if he told Auntie Sandra what had really happened but she didn't send for a doctor to see me so I think she must have known and been afraid that a doctor would discover the truth. I think my form teacher was suspicious about the story. She asked me what had happened but I was too scared to tell her. Who would believe my word against that of a respectable man like him? And if they didn't believe me they would tell Uncle John what I had said about him...

I never threw the discus again. When I tried it I discovered I couldn't lift my arm high enough – so there must have been some damage done inside but I never found out what it was. Anyway, I learned my lesson. It wasn't enough to keep out of Uncle John's way. I would have to obey the rules too. I had less than two years to go before I left the home so I decided to keep my nose clean from then on, otherwise the next time I 'fell down the stairs' I had a feeling I might break my neck.

8

In the summer of 1967, just after my sixteenth birthday, I took my O-level examinations and was told in August that I had passed in six subjects: English language, English literature, art, craft, biology and domestic science – so I wasn't so dumb. When the results were out, the employment officer came round and gave us interviews.

'You've done well,' he said to me. 'You could get a good job. What would you like to do?'

This was where I made my big mistake. I asked if he could get me a job as a lion-tamer. He laughed, which upset me. I said I didn't see why he thought it was so funny and eventually he realized I was completely serious. It was what I had dreamed of since I first started thinking about what I was going to be when I grew up. Nursing, teaching and all the other careers that are supposed to appeal to little girls had never held any attraction for me.

'Well,' he said doubtfully, 'I suppose I could get you a job at Chester Zoo cleaning out the animals.'

'Do you mind?' I said. 'I don't want to be cleaning cages out.'

For years I had cherished this romantic vision of myself in a sparkling suit and top hat putting lions and tigers through their paces and bowing to the applause of the crowd. Shovelling manure definitely didn't fit in with my fantasy.

After that the employment officer seemed to lose interest in me. He was used to the sort of people who said they wanted to be hairdressers or shop assistants.

It was decided that I should be a mother's help and they found me a job with a family on a farm. I suppose they thought that cows were as close to lions as they could get. I don't know who took the final decision but I didn't have much say in the matter. I

77

wasn't bothered, though. I was sixteen and I was leaving the home. That was all that I cared about.

But I was rejoicing too soon. After a week on the farm I came back to the home with my tail between my legs. As a nanny I was a total failure. It wasn't all my fault. I think the woman I'd been working for was suffering from post-natal depression. At any rate, she had a small baby as well as two older children and was in a terribly nervous state. She used to cry a lot and go to bed and leave me to sort the kids out. I didn't often see her husband. He was a jazz player with a group and was away nearly every night I was there.

On top of that the place turned out not to be a proper farm at all, just an old farmhouse that they'd done up fashionably, so I didn't even have any animals to make the job more pleasant.

I couldn't cope with the situation. I was only sixteen – still a kid myself – and I just wasn't mature enough to take care of three small children. I'd been thrown from one extreme to another. I'd come from an institution where I wasn't allowed to sneeze without permission into this house where I was being offered cigarettes and left to do what I wanted. I started smoking all day and the kids ran riot because I couldn't control them.

I felt a real failure when I walked back up the drive to the home, though I feel now that I'd simply been expected to grow up too quickly.

It took them another week to decide what to do with me, but they worked hard on it. Uncle John didn't want me around a moment longer than I had to be. I suppose every time he looked at me he was reminded of what could happen to him if I spilled the beans about him, but in any case once I'd left school I wasn't supposed to stay in the home any longer – it was one of the rules.

The solution they came up with was that I should be sent to a halfway house. This was a sort of launching pad into the big wide world for kids who had been long-term in children's homes and was meant to prepare you gently for living outside an institution. I don't know why I wasn't sent there in the first place. Given that I'd spent over eight years in an institution they might have guessed that I'd find it difficult to adapt to anything else.

In preparation for my release into 'normal society' Auntie Sandra decided to get me a complete new outfit and took me shopping with her in Liverpool. I remember she bought me a mustard coat, some cerise shoes with black laces and a blue and white polka-dot skirt. Tasteful colour schemes weren't her strong point.

I wanted a dress as well but she said the allowance wouldn't stretch to that, so she bought some material instead and said she would make me a tent dress. They were all the rage then, but I wasn't very grateful for it. Auntie Sandra wasn't the best needlewoman in the world and I wanted a proper shop dress.

Maybe I sulked on the way back or did something else to upset her, I don't remember. What I do remember is that when we got back to the home that evening all the other children were preparing to go on their weekly trip to the swimming baths but when I ran to get my costume Auntie Sandra called me back and said I couldn't go because I'd already had my outing that day. I wasn't to be allowed two treats even if I was sixteen.

When I had first come to the home at the age of eight, a Mr Woolridge had been appointed as my welfare officer. He was the grey-haired man who had first visited me in Western Avenue to ask me if I'd like a holiday. What being a welfare officer meant as far as I could see was that once or twice a year he'd come to the home and have tea with the staff in the best front room and hear from them how they thought I was doing. It didn't seem to involve asking me for my opinion on the matter. After a few years Mr Woolridge retired and was replaced by Mrs Crystal, who was younger and quite pretty; but there was no change in the way she looked after my welfare. She used to have long discussions with the Englishes behind closed doors and afterwards she could come and say hello to me with them looking on but she never had the chance to get to know me on my own. I don't think she ever spoke to me without their being there too. And I think this was why I never thought of going to my welfare officer when anything bad happened at the home. In my mind she was one of them – on the side of the authorities, not on my side at all.

So on the day I was due to leave it was Mrs Crystal who had the job of taking me from the home to the halfway house. She drove up in her estate car and loaded me and my luggage inside. I had one suitcase which contained every possession I had and £16 in cash, which I'd saved from my pocket money. I was quite a thrifty kid.

Now that the day had finally arrived I felt strange. Of course I was excited but at the same time I was frightened. Whenever I'd looked forward to a change in the past it had turned out not to be for the better. What if the halfway house turned out to be even worse than the home? I said goodbye to Alan first and said not to cry, I'd see him when I visited Thelma in Liverpool. He looked sad, as though he didn't believe me, and I had to walk away quickly before I started crying myself. Then I said goodbye to the girls with whom I'd shared a bedroom and for a few moments I felt really depressed. I knew that this time, whatever happened, I wouldn't be coming back so it was probably the last time I'd ever see Shirley and Mona and the others.

The worst part was saying goodbye to Auntie Angela, but I think she knew how I was feeling and she tried to cheer me up by saying she'd come to see me if she went to Liverpool. Then Mrs Crystal called from the front door that she was ready to go and I turned and went before Auntie Angela could see me crying. Uncle John and Auntie Sandra came to the car with me and smiled false smiles as I climbed in.

'Goodbye, Gloria,' they said. 'Look after yourself.'

I think all I said in reply was 'Goodbye'. I didn't know how to begin to say all the things I wanted to say, all the things I maybe should have said to them, so I said nothing.

Then the car swung away over the gravel drive and as the trees closed in behind us I didn't once look back. My tears of a few moments before were forgotten and I felt like a canary whose cage door had been opened. It had been silly to be afraid of the future. I felt a sudden glow of confidence and excitement. Whatever happened to me now could never be as bad as what had happened to me in there. My life from now on was going to be all right. I knew it.

PART 2

9

The halfway house turned out to be an ordinary-looking terraced house in the centre of Birkenhead. That was the first good thing about it. I'd had enough of living in a spooky mansion. Mrs Crystal took me in, introduced me and showed me round. Before she left she gave me her phone number and told me to call her if I wanted her. She said she was still my welfare officer even though I had left the children's home and it was her job to keep an eye on me and help me out if I needed it.

The second good thing about my new home at 19 Elm Road North was that there were only six girls there including me, so it felt much more as though I were in a family than when I had been one of 26 children. The other girls had come from children's homes as well and were all more or less the same age as me. We slept two to a bedroom instead of in a dormitory and I was given a room with a girl from London called Pat. We got on with each other straight away and over the next few weeks we became good friends and started going everywhere together.

The woman who ran the home was called Mrs Roberts. Like the Englishes, she had her own family living with her, which I didn't think was a good idea. It meant once again the home was divided into 'them' and 'us', and like kids everywhere in institutions we always felt that 'they' had a better life than we did. They certainly ate better: *that* wasn't just imagination. All Mrs Roberts' family ate in their own dining room and they used to have steaks and roasts while we were having poached egg and baked beans.

We had to call Mrs Roberts 'Mum', which I didn't like doing, but apart from that she was all right. She was an improvement on Auntie Sandra anyway. She looked a bit funny though. 'Vivid' is the word I think of when I remember her now: bleached hair, bright red lipstick, brilliant green eye-shadow... The biggest thing in her favour from my point of view was that she left us alone and wasn't always interfering in our lives. As long as we didn't cause her any trouble she was happy.

I drove her crazy for the first few weeks I was there because I couldn't get used to being allowed out without permission. I would go and knock on her door all the time and after a bit she'd get really irritable when she saw it was me.

'Yes, what is it, Gloria? What now?'

'Can I go out, please?' I'd say.

'Yes, of course you can. What are you asking me for? I've told you that you don't have to ask me.'

But after eight years it was hard to change. If I'd been given a bit more responsibility in my last year at the home it would have been easier, but I had been treated like a small child right up until the day I left and then, overnight it seemed to me, I was expected to behave like a grown-up.

We had to pay Mrs Roberts rent money of £7 a week, and for that we got our room, our food and our laundry done. She didn't put herself out too much over our food. Fish and chips was the most popular supper with her, because there was a chippie just around the corner, and baked beans were her favourite vegetable. I still hate baked beans all these years after Mrs Roberts stuffed us full of them.

The first week I was there I was found a job. Any thought of careers guidance seemed to have ended now I'd left the home and it seemed that none of the other girls had been given any choice about what they did either. The result was that all of us were found jobs in a laundry in Birkenhead. Whether we were bright or dim, good at maths or fond of cooking, it didn't seem to matter. As far as the people in charge were concerned, we were the kids from the home and we could work in the laundry. That, at any rate, is the way their attitude appeared to us.

I absolutely hated it. It was the most boring job on earth: we spent most of the day folding up wet sheets. I soon said to myself, 'Gloria, this is not your calling.'

It wasn't just that it was hard work. I wasn't afraid of hard work, but it was so mindless. It wasn't enough for my brain. I was intelligent enough to get six O-levels but this was like being put back into the D form at school.

We used to make extra toast in the mornings at the halfway house and take it in with us to eat for lunch. There was a canteen at work but it was expensive and we only used to eat there once or twice most weeks. On the other days at lunchtime we'd sit around on a bench outside the laundry munching our toast and moaning about how much we hated the job.

After three months of moaning I decided it was time to do something about it, so I asked Mrs Crystal if she could help find me another job. To my delight she managed to get me a place in a hairdresser's salon quite quickly, but my pleasure didn't last long. I soon discovered I couldn't stand it. It was nearly as bad as folding sheets. I was an apprentice, which meant that all I was allowed to do was shampoo hair and sweep floors. I never even got any tips. After a week my hands were soggy and sore and my brain started to rebel.

The worst part was having to treat the customers as though they were gods. I'd soon had enough of all that and I think it must have showed. Customers started to complain about me – once it was because I'd eaten a cheese-and-raw-onion sandwich at lunchtime and one of them said my breath smelled of onion and made her feel ill. Another time I accidentally hit someone over the head with a hairbrush which I was waving to try to get one of the girls to bring me the conditioner.

I knew it was only a matter of time before I got the sack but I didn't care very much. Gradually other things were becoming more important to me than work – like friends and having a good time.

For although hairdressing had been a disaster my social life was now a raging success. As there was so little control over when I came and went I started spending more and more time hanging round in town with the other girls, especially Pat. In any case, we weren't allowed to stay in the halfway house on our days off from work. We had to get out after breakfast as Mrs Roberts said she didn't want us under her feet. We used to sit around in coffee bars in the daytime and every evening, whether or not it had been a working day, we'd go to the pictures or to a disco or to a pub.

We soon found that being only sixteen years old was no obstacle to getting drinks if you put a bit of make-up on your face. We discovered alcohol and boys at about the same time, though at this stage the boyfriends weren't serious, mainly because we had to be back in the halfway house by 11 o'clock, when Mrs Roberts locked the door. So there was no opportunity for anything more wicked than a quick kissing session on the way home from the pub to Elm Road North and most of us remained pretty innocent for girls of sixteen.

I used to go over the water to Liverpool quite often to stay with my sister Joyce, who by now had five children. My mother was living just around the corner from Joyce but I never went to see her. I blamed her for putting me in the home. If I saw her in the street or if she ever came to Joyce's house I just used to ignore her. I felt she was a stranger.

By Christmas 1967 I'd been at Birkenhead six months. I didn't know what to do to celebrate my first Christmas of 'freedom'. Joyce's husband had started objecting to my spending so much time there. He and Joyce weren't getting on too well and he could get a bit violent when he'd been drinking. Joyce told me she was sorry but she didn't dare ask me over for Christmas dinner. I had to find somewhere to go, though, because the halfway house was closing down for a few days over Christmas, so I arranged to stay with my sister Thelma, who was now living in Birmingham.

I planned to leave on Christmas Eve and as Pat was going to London at the same time we decided to go to the pub together at lunchtime on Christmas Eve for a few drinks first. We took our suitcases with us with the intention of going straight on to Lime Street Station after an hour or so.

I suppose it was predictable that we should get completely tipsy and miss our trains. I remember drinking weird mixtures and people in the pub buying us drinks one after another and kissing us under the mistletoe – and then me suddenly looking at my watch and shrieking, 'Let's go!' and us racing to the ferry and then leaping on to a bus with our cases and half an hour later dashing on to the platform at Lime Street just as the Birmingham train was pulling out. Pat's train had left ten minutes before. They were the last trains for three days.

When we sobered up enough to realize the mess we were in, I remembered that Mrs Crystal was working over Christmas at a children's home in Liverpool as a relief matron.

We found our way there and confessed what had happened. Mrs Crystal shook her head at us and drove us back to Mrs Roberts' in Birkenhead. There she explained the situation and said that she was afraid we would just have to stay at the halfway house over Christmas. By now it was about 6 o'clock in the evening. Mrs Roberts listened silently while Mrs Crystal talked to her but as soon as she left she laid into us. She was furious.

She said we'd ruined her Christmas. It was her holiday too, she said. She didn't want to have to look after us when she was supposed to be relaxing with her family. She did enough of that all the rest of the year. In any case she didn't have enough food to give us Christmas dinner as well as feed her own family, though she didn't expect thoughtless girls like us to think about things like that. She went on and on getting madder and madder at us until finally she ran out of things to say and sent us to bed without any supper.

'And don't bother getting up in the morning,' she yelled up the stairs after us. 'You can forget about your Christmas dinner. You can forget about Christmas altogether. I don't want to see either of you again until Boxing Day' – and with that she went back into her own living room and slammed the door behind her.

Pat looked at me and shrugged and went into our bedroom, but I couldn't accept what Mrs Roberts had just said. All the happiness and excitement that had filled me earlier in the day had disappeared like a balloon popping. I felt suddenly betrayed. I had thought I was free and now it was as though I was back in the home again, where I was always getting into trouble – often without even realizing I had done anything wrong. It had been like playing a never-ending game of snakes and ladders, except that there were hardly any ladders but millions of snakes. And now I was back in the game.

We hadn't set out to cause trouble that afternoon. Missing the train had been an accident. We had both been looking forward to spending Christmas with our families, opening presents, eating turkey and pulling crackers, so to find all at once that Christmas Day was being taken from me as a punishment for having a good time at the pub was too much for me. Whenever I enjoyed myself it seemed I always had to pay for it afterwards. It wasn't fair. I felt all at once that my whole life had been unfair. A terrific anger, unlike anything I'd ever experienced before, surged inside me. I felt as though I were going to explode.

Instead, I rushed to the bathroom and drank two cups of Vim and water. It sounds funny now, but it was all I could find. If there'd been any tablets or razors I'd have used them but the only useful item in the bathroom was a pack of Vim, so that's what I took. If anyone had asked me why, I couldn't have explained it. All I knew was that this rage was bursting inside me and this was how I tried to let it out.

It did me no good. I lay on the bed for two hours burping bubbles. I didn't tell Pat what I'd done. When it became obvious to me that I wasn't going to die I decided to run away and try to get to Thelma's house anyway, train or no train.

Pat was asleep at about 9 o'clock that evening when I sneaked out of the house with my suitcase and made my way down to the ferry. Once over the river I got a bus up to the East Lancs. Road and started hitching down the motorway to Birmingham. I'd never hitched before, but maybe because it was Christmas and people were feeling Christian I didn't have any trouble getting lifts. I had two nasty moments, though. The first came soon after I started out.

One of my lifts dropped me off at a roundabout and I walked on up the road in the dark with my thumb stuck out. I was such a novice I didn't even know it was illegal to hitch on motorways.

The next thing I knew a white car pulled on to the hard shoulder in front of me and two policemen got out.

My heart nearly stopped. I felt sure they were looking for me and would take me back, but no, they just explained I was breaking the law. They seemed full of Christmas spirit as well and they gave me a lift back off the motorway to the next roundabout.

Then, when I was nearly in Birmingham, I was picked up by a grey-haired man in an old clapped-out car. We'd only just set off when his hand left the gear-stick and started stroking my leg. I kept pushing it away, and then, luckily for me, he had to stop at some traffic lights so I jumped out, my opinion of men in general dropping yet another notch.

By this time I was in the outskirts of Birmingham and I decided to walk the rest of the way rather than risk meeting any more weirdos.

It was nearly 3 o'clock on Christmas morning when I finally knocked on Thelma's door. She had been living for the last eight years with an African from Gambia called David and the house was full of his friends, who were in the middle of a noisy party. Thelma looked surprised to see me when she opened the door because Mrs Crystal had phoned her to say I wasn't coming after all. She wasn't too pleased when she heard that I'd run away.

'Oh, Gloria! What have you gone and done a thing like that for?' she sighed, as though I were nothing but trouble. I wondered why I'd bothered coming.

'Oh, go on,' I begged. 'Let me stay. I'll do your cooking for you. I'll be a real help, honest. I've got presents for all the kids.'

I could be really pathetic when I tried and at that moment I felt more pathetic than ever in my life.

Thelma looked at me and I could see she was thinking about it. Then she smiled and my heart rose.

'All right then,' she agreed. 'You can stay as long as you can get away with it. But I bet the police will be here by tomorrow.'

They were, too. They knocked on the door at nine in the morning. Thelma rushed me round the back to her next-door neighbour and I hid in her coalshed, trembling, while Thelma told the police she hadn't seen me for six months but would let them know if I turned up. They told her that Mrs Roberts had reported me missing and was worried about me.

When the police had gone away Thelma asked me what I intended doing and if I was going back to live with Mrs Roberts after Christmas.

'Are you kidding?' I said. 'Nothing'll make me go back to that place.'

'Well, you can't stay here,' said Thelma. 'I don't want the police back here again. We'll have to think of something.'

That night, Thelma and David took me to a big Christmas dance in Birmingham and there David introduced me to two of his African friends who had come up from London. They seemed quite friendly and while they were chatting to Thelma and me Thelma told them I wanted to leave Birmingham and they asked me why I didn't go to London. So on the spur of the moment I decided that was what I would do.

It seemed after all the obvious place to go to when you wanted to disappear. And I *did* want to disappear. I realized that when I thought about it. I'd had enough of Mrs Roberts and Birkenhead and hairdressing. I hadn't waited all those years at the home hoping for this sort of life at the end of it. I'd pictured glamour and excitement and foreign travel as my future but I wasn't going to find any of that at the halfway house. I'd never been to London but it held the same fascination for me that it did for most teenagers. As soon as it was suggested I wondered why it hadn't occurred to me before.

The two men said they were going back to London on Boxing Day and could give me a lift if I wanted. The main problem I faced would be getting out of the house, because Thelma reckoned that the police would be watching for me outside; but we decided to risk it.

The next afternoon Dave's two African friends arrived outside Thelma's house in a red Mini and while Thelma looked out for me I ran out of the front door. One of the guys got out and held the car door open for me while I scrambled into the back and lay down on the floor. Then the man got back into the front passenger seat and leaned over and pulled a rug over me in case the police were watching. While he was doing this, Thelma put my case in the boot and before she could even say goodbye we drove off.

After half an hour, just when I thought I was going to die from lack of oxygen, the fellows in the front of the car tapped me through the blanket and told me it was all clear. I stuck my head up to find we were on the motorway.

I pulled myself up on to the back seat and started to think what my next move would be. All I had in my purse was £10, which even I knew wouldn't get me very far in London, but as it turned out the decision, for that night anyway, was taken out of my hands.

The two men ignored me and gabbled away to each other all the way down the motorway. They were quite young – in their twenties, I guessed. I don't know whether it was their accents or if they were talking an African language, but most of the time I couldn't understand a word of what they were saying. Eventually they seemed to agree something between themselves and the one who wasn't driving turned round and spoke to me.

'We're going to take you to a club,' he said. 'Show you a bit of London. Look after you like your sister told us to.'

I didn't want to be looked after. Not by these two, anyway – they were beginning to make me feel nervous, the way they were looking at me – but I was trapped.

They took me to a club and all the time I was there, sipping orange juice and watching them knock back whisky, I was thinking of ways I could shake them loose. I said I wanted to go to the ladies' room and while I was there a girl came in. I waited till she was combing her hair and checking her make-up in the mirror, then I went up to her and tried to explain the situation, which wasn't easy in the time I had available. I told her, truthfully, that I was frightened of the men.

'If you could come up to us and pretend that you know me I think I can get away from them,' I told her.

I must have convinced her I was genuine because she did as I'd asked and tried to persuade them we were old friends, but they were pretty wise, these guys, and they hung on to me – I mean physically hung on, till my arms felt they were black and blue. They told the girl to clear off, which she did, with a shrug of the shoulders to me to tell me she'd done her best. I began to feel really scared.

When the show was over the men pushed me back in the Mini, ignoring my protests, and drove me to a flat. I sat in the kitchen with them and they stayed up drinking for a while and then the big guy, the one who'd driven down, left and I was alone with the other one. He'd had a lot to drink but his eyes were bright and glittery and he was looking at me the way a cat looks at a mouse. I think I knew then what was going to happen. He reminded me of the way Uncle John had looked that night he had dragged me out of the bath.

'I'll sleep on the chair,' I said, without much hope.

'No, no. You go to bed in there,' Dave's friend said, pointing to the bedroom door. I did as he told me, taking my suitcase with me, and shut the door behind me. In the room were a wardrobe, a dressing-table and a double bed. Quickly I put my nightdress on, switched the light off and slid under the covers of the bed.

A few minutes later the door opened and he came in. I pretended to be asleep but it was no good. He stood in the dark beside the bed and I heard his clothes drop to the floor, then without saying a word he climbed in beside me and put his arms round me. I turned away from him and made snoring noises but he wasn't fooled. His hands crept over my breasts then moved down between my legs. Then, roughly, he pulled me over to face him again, pinned my shoulders down and pulled himself on top of me.

As rapes go, I suppose it wasn't as violent as it might have been, because once I realized there was no point resisting him I just lay there and let it happen. I knew he was twice as strong as me and there was no one to help even if I had screamed and kicked up a fuss, so I just lay there rigid and prayed for it to be over soon.

As it turned out I wasn't even granted that wish. Probably because of all the booze he'd had, it seemed to go on for ever with him grunting and sweating on top of me in the dark. Then at last, just when I thought I was going to suffocate with his weight and the beer fumes, he collapsed and rolled off me, and in a few minutes he was asleep, his face buried in the pillow beside me.

I slid off the bed, picked my clothes and suitcase up off the floor and crept to the door. In the kitchen I opened my suitcase and rummaged through it for some clean underwear. I wasn't crying. I didn't feel hysterical the way some people say they feel when they've been raped. I just felt sick and sort of cold inside. I raked through my case, trying to find my clothes by touch because I was afraid to put the light on. Then all at once I stopped as a thought struck me.

Where was I going to go in the middle of the night. The police? Back to the home? Out on to the street? I felt sick and hurt and disgusted but whatever I'd been afraid of had already happened and there was no changing it. It was over and it wasn't going to happen again while he lay in that drunken sleep.

I made myself a cup of tea in the next room while I thought about what to do, then I came back into the bedroom, picked my nightdress up off the floor and put it back on. I climbed back into the bed as far from the snoring body and the wet patch on the sheet as I could get, and after a bit I fell asleep too.

When I awoke the next morning it was light and the man lay next to me in the bed still unconscious, with his mouth open, and his arms flung out. I decided that if I was going then now was the time to go. His eyes opened as I got out of the bed and he grunted at me and asked me what I was doing. I thought quickly.

'I'm just going to the shops for some milk to make some tea,' I answered.

'Fetch some fags as well. There's some money in my pocket,' he said and he turned over and started to snore again.

I found a £5 note in the pocket of his jeans, which still lay on the floor where he'd dropped them the night before. I dressed, picked my case up and crept out, with his fiver in my hand. When I got out of the front door I ran as fast as I ever remember running, up the street and round the corner. Half-way down the next road there was a bus-stop with a big red London bus standing waiting to pull out. It said 'Chelsea' on the front. I hadn't a clue where Chelsea was, but it sounded all right to me so I tore across the road and leaped on board just as it moved off.

I told the conductor I wanted to go as far as the bus went and twenty minutes later he put me off at a bus-stop in Chelsea. All I could think of was that I was gasping for a cup of tea, so I went into a snack bar over the road from the bus-stop and sat down. A waitress brought me a pot of tea. It was that sort of snack bar, not self-service as I was used to. The waitress looked at me as though she thought I didn't belong there, and I couldn't blame her: I must have looked a wreck. I hadn't combed my hair or anything before I'd bolted from the house, and I was still feeling stunned by what had happened in the last 48 hours. I sat and stared down at my tea and wondered what I was going to do now. I felt as close to praying as I had ever done since my days in the Salvation Army.

But it was just a moment later, before I'd even started saying prayers, that the best piece of good luck I'd ever had in my life came my way. For it was then, as I peered up from my drink at the customers sitting at the other tables, that I met Miranda.

10

She was sitting at the table next to me, a smartly dressed woman of about 25, pretty and made-up like a fashion model. To her, I must have looked like something the cat brought in, and perhaps because of that she seemed fascinated by me. I kept glancing up to find her staring at me, and then, as I took a sideways peep at her, and before I could look away again, she smiled.

'Hello,' she said.

She had a voice that nowadays you'd say was Sloane Ranger, but then I just thought she sounded kind. I muttered hello back to her and she smiled again.

'Are you all right?' she asked. 'You don't look very well.'

If she'd said something rude or unpleasant to me I'd just have sworn at her and thought no more of it, but kindness was more than I could bear. Great big tears started to roll down my cheeks, on to my nose and into my tea.

She sat down opposite me, took my hand and held it and the tears flowed faster – great streams of them, trickling down my face and splashing on to the table. My nose was running too. I started to sniff and of course I had nothing to blow my nose on. Getting dressed that morning hadn't included putting a hankie up my sleeve. She passed me a serviette to wipe my nose with and sat there holding my hand and gently asking me questions and bit by bit I told her my story.

It sounds odd even to me now that I confessed all to a complete stranger but it seemed natural then. Something told me that this was a person I could trust – and my instinct was right, as I found out later.

She didn't say anything while I was talking, except to ask a short question here and there and to nod sympathetically in the right places. When I'd finished my story she still didn't speak for a while, then she asked where I was planning to go next. That set me off in tears again as I hadn't a clue.

She looked thoughtful for a minute before saying, 'Gloria, how would you like to come and stay in my flat for a while until you sort things out?'

I couldn't believe it. I'd met some nice people during my time at the home, it was true, and along the way lots of people had done nice things for me, but it had never put them out too much. It was always just a kind gesture now and then – a day-trip or a visit, something that didn't require too much commitment from them.

Now here was a total stranger offering to take me into her life – and a stranger who knew the police were looking for me, so she too could have got into trouble. I decided I had met a real live saint. I often think about her today and I still feel the same way about her.

It turned out she was an air stewardess living in an attic flat in Earl's Court. I went back to her home with her and the first thing she did was to take my case from me and lead me into her bathroom, which was pink and feminine and perfumed. Then she ran me a bath and said I was to stay there as long as I wanted. Meanwhile, she would make some lunch for me. She seemed to understand how dirty I felt without my telling her and she did all the right things. After I'd bathed and eaten we sat and talked about life and men and what had happened to me and gradually some of the pain started to go away.

I told her not to worry about the police being after me because I hadn't done anything wrong except to run away after being sent to bed on Christmas Eve. She laughed and said she believed me.

I said I'd help her with the cooking while I stayed there – I told her about my O-level in cookery – and I'd do the cleaning and look after the flat while she was away on foreign flights. We were like two kids planning an adventure.

It was like heaven, the five weeks I stayed with Miranda in her flat – like playing at house when you're growing up. She had a really pretty flat, all beautifully decorated and furnished – not with terribly expensive things, but tastefully, which made a great impression on me. It was the first time I'd lived in a tastefully decorated place in my life.

It was a problem not having any money coming in, but I was able to get by without it because in return for my keeping the flat tidy and doing the cooking Miranda and her boyfriend would take me out with them. After we'd had dinner in the evening we'd go to the cinema or to parties. Sometimes I'd borrow Miranda's clothes. Miranda's boyfriend, Patrick, was nice too, though he must have got fed up with me tagging along playing gooseberry everywhere they went.

'Oh. Are we taking *her* along again?' he'd say with a wink at me to show he didn't mean it.

'Aw, shurrup, Patrick,' I'd answer in my broadest Liverpool accent – it hadn't taken me long to get rid of my Chester twang – 'I cooked you a nice dinner tonight so shurrup and take me out.'

Patrick was very posh and well-educated but Miranda used to stick up for me so I felt all right cheeking him and taking the mickey. I was becoming a bit of a hard case by now – on the surface, anyway – and they can't have come across anyone in their lives like me before. Their childhood had been a world of private schools and *au pairs* and holidays abroad, but they seemed to accept me for what I was and I never felt that they were prejudiced because of my background. For instance, although she knew I hadn't any money Miranda would leave her purse, cheque book and jewellery around knowing that at any minute I could have cleared off with them. The fact that she trusted me enough to do that made me feel six feet tall.

I was introduced to their whole circle of friends. Patrick had a sister with whom I got on really well. On New Year's Day they took me to a party at Patrick's godmother's house. It was a really smart affair, with the women in long dresses and the men in dinner-jackets. I couldn't believe it. From being a nobody who a few months before had been folding wet sheets in Birkenhead I was suddenly mixing with London's beautiful people, drinking exotic cocktails and being asked to dance by good-looking men who didn't have pimples. It felt like winning the pools.

I had spent five weeks in the flat and had no thought of ever leaving it when one afternoon, bored with hanging around on my own while Miranda was working, I decided to go to Heathrow Airport to meet her when she came off her flight.

I was still hooked on the idea of travel and flying, so just being at the airport was a thrill for me. Miranda's plane was due in at 4 o'clock but I arrived at two and wandered around drinking in the atmosphere. All the old memories of Speke Airport came back and I felt like a little girl again, looking at the planes taking off. Then over the loudspeakers they announced that Miranda's flight had been delayed by an hour and as I was at a loose end I decided on the spur of the moment to ring Mrs Roberts. I knew she'd probably have been worrying about me over the last weeks and I thought I'd let her know I was all right. I had to go through the operator to get the home's number. Mrs Roberts answered the phone herself.

'Mum?' I said. 'It's me, Gloria. I'm ringing to let you know I'm OK.'

'Gloria?' she said, her voice sharp and anxious. 'Where have you been? Where are you?'

'I'm in Manchester,' I said, thinking quickly. 'Don't worry. I'm all right.'

And then the operator cut in – she must have been listening in and had worked out the situation.

'You bad girl!' she said. 'Why don't you tell her the truth – that you're at London Heathrow?'

'Because I didn't want her to know I was here!' I yelled, outraged, and slammed the phone down.

I couldn't believe it. How dare some complete stranger interfere in my life? I went into the cafeteria. It was still half an hour before Miranda's flight was due in. I decided to risk it and wait for her. Surely they wouldn't have time to send out a search party for me in that short time. I was wrong. Twenty minutes later as I sat trying to look invisible, two policemen picked me up.

'Gloria Lovatt?' they said.

'Who – me?' I said.

'Come off it, Gloria.' They were smiling. They knew it was me. Mrs Roberts must have given them a good description, though she can't have known what I was wearing as I had some of Miranda's clothes on. Anyway, the game was up.

'That's it,' I thought. 'Never again will I let my stupid conscience make me do something so dumb.' If I hadn't worried about Mrs Roberts' feelings I might have got away with my disappearance forever – or at least till I was eighteen, when it wouldn't have mattered any more.

I persuaded the policemen to wait for Miranda and at last her flight came in. When she saw the policemen she weighed up the situation straight away. She told them I'd been living with her since I'd run away.

'She's all right. She's been a good girl,' she said. 'She hasn't been in any trouble.'

'Thanks a lot. You make me sound like a pet cat,' I said. I was trying to joke my way through it but really I felt torn apart at the thought of leaving Miranda and I think she realized it.

'She doesn't have to go back to Liverpool this minute, does she?' Miranda pleaded. 'All her things are at my place. Give her a chance to pack.'

No one else could have wangled it but they were like putty in Miranda's hands. I don't know if it was her accent or her attitude which persuaded them it was OK, but they agreed I could go back to her flat as long as we gave them the address, which we did. But I was only buying time.

The next morning Miranda's doorbell rang and standing outside was my welfare officer, Mrs Crystal.

'Hello, Gloria.' She had this all-weather smile and she gave me the full benefit of it. I got the feeling that behind her stretched lips, her teeth were gritted. Miranda asked her in.

'Listen, Mrs Crystal,' I said desperately, 'I'm happy where I am. There's no point me going back. It'll only make more work for you.'

She shook her head wearily. 'Come on, Gloria – you know the

rules. You're in our care until you're eighteen. Then you can come back if you still want to.' The way she said it suggested that I wouldn't still want to when I'd come to my senses.

I retorted angrily, 'You bet I will. Nothing will stop me coming back here.'

Miranda helped me pack my suitcase, hugged me goodbye and wished me luck, and together Mrs Crystal and I walked to the station to catch the train back to Liverpool.

That should have been the end of the story for that day. To my mind it was enough to lose my new home and new friends and new way of life all in one go, without having anything else happening. But Fate had another card up her sleeve for me. As we were going along the pavement Mrs Crystal noticed I was walking in a funny way.

She stopped in her tracks and looked suspiciously at me.

'What's wrong with you, Gloria?'

'What do you mean? What's the matter now?' I asked sulkily.

'You look uncomfortable – as though it hurts when you walk.'

'It's nothing,' I said, embarrassed that she should have noticed. 'It's just that I've got these sores at the tops of my legs and with you making me walk so fast they're rubbing together.'

I hadn't told Miranda about the sores. I hadn't thought it was important. I'd first noticed them a couple of weeks after I arrived in London. I'd thought maybe it was just another part of being a teenager, like getting spots.

Mrs Crystal gave me a knowing look.

'I think we'd better get you to a doctor when we get back to Birkenhead,' she said.

I wasn't particularly bothered about the sores and I told her not to fuss, but she made me an appointment anyway, as soon as we got off the train.

When she got me to the surgery the doctor took one look at the sores and quickly told me to get dressed again. Mrs Crystal had stayed with me while I was examined and the doctor ignored me and spoke to her as he washed his hands.

'Yes, you're quite right. She appears to be suffering from gonorrhoea,' he said.

I wasn't having this – their talking over my head.

'What's that you said I've got?' I interrupted.

He didn't seem to have heard me. Mrs Crystal answered for him.

'It's something you get when you're promiscuous, Gloria. When you sleep around with lots of men.' She looked cross and disapproving.

As the penny dropped I opened my mouth to protest. I wanted them to know that I hadn't been promiscuous, I'd been raped, but after a quick look at both their faces I decided not to bother. In their eyes I was a dog with a bad name, a child in care – an absconder. Of course they thought I slept around. It all fitted in with the rest of the picture they had of me. The doctor prescribed me some medication and I left the surgery with Mrs Crystal.

Mrs Roberts wouldn't take me back into the halfway house. I don't know if it was because I had caught VD or because I'd run away, but she didn't want me, so they stuck me in the Falconer House Reform School in Liverpool. It was an awful place, really bad. If it had been where ordinary people lived it would have been called a slum. The paintwork was all old and peeling and the furniture was scruffy and falling apart. The girls all slept together in big dormitories so there was no privacy at all.

The inmates of the reform school weren't like the girls I'd known in the home or the halfway house. They were hard and unfriendly towards me, and they seemed a lot older, even though I don't suppose any of them was more than twenty. But all of them had been in trouble with the police, mostly for things a lot more serious than just running away. I felt that by being put with them I too was being labelled a criminal, and this upset me.

There wasn't much to do while we were there. Of course there was no question of my getting a job while I was considered at risk of absconding again, so to fill in the time while the other girls were watching TV I started to write a book of animal stories. I got quite enthusiastic about it. All the tales I'd woven in my head in the days when Uncle John used to lock me in the broom cupboard with the *Jungle Book* came flooding back to me, and I spent hours scribbling in red exercise books. Over the next few weeks I filled about ten of them.

I missed Miranda terribly while I was at the reform school. I felt that she had been my first real friend, the first person who had really cared for me and liked me for what I was. She had never tried to change me or lecture me about my faults like everyone else, and I loved her for that. I spent most of my time when I wasn't writing my book thinking about how I could get back to her.

There were two girls at the reform school that I got to know quite well. If I'd known then what I found out later I wouldn't have called them friends, but in my ignorance that's what I thought they were. A few weeks after I'd arrived at Falconer House they decided to run away so I said I'd go with them, being an expert in doing a bunk by this time and prepared to act as their adviser in return for their company.

I had some beautiful clothes by now – they were beautiful to my eyes, anyway. Some I'd saved up for and bought while I was at Mrs Roberts' and they'd been sent on to the reform school from the halfway house, and some Miranda had given me: there was no way I was going to leave them behind, so I packed them all into two suitcases. Then one morning the other girls and I just got up early and walked out of the back door.

Naturally we were aiming for London and we got a ride on two trucks as we couldn't all fit into one, especially with all my luggage. The other girls took the first truck which stopped and left me on my own to try to find another one. We'd arranged to meet at a service station half-way down the motorway. I had no trouble getting a lift and I arrived at the service station about half an hour after the other two. But by now another problem was bothering me.

I was still taking medication for the gonorrhoea but I had forgotten to bring it with me and I'd missed my morning dose. By the time I got out of the truck I wasn't feeling too well. I had a drink of orange juice and told the girls I was getting cramps in my stomach. They said I'd be all right after a drink and a rest. But I wasn't. The pain started to get worse and I had to go to the bathroom. I spent about ten minutes doubled up over the toilet, then, realizing that if I was going to get to London at all I was going to have to pull myself together, I hobbled back into the café.

The girls had gone, and with them they'd taken my suitcases. All I could think about at first was my lovely clothes, then I remembered that I'd packed my book of animal stories as well. I'd been up to chapter 25. For a moment I felt like crying. Then the pain in my stomach came back and I forgot about everything but getting to Miranda's. I felt she was the only one who could help me.

My truck driver said he didn't know where the two girls were heading but they'd left in the other lorry and they'd told him a story that I'd asked them to look after my suitcases, so he'd handed them over. I decided I had no choice but to get back in my truck and head for London on my own.

But it wasn't meant to be. We'd got about 50 miles down the motorway when the pain low down in my belly became unbearable and I asked the driver to find me a hospital. I thought I was dying. The driver was very good. He drove me into some town – I forget now where it was – and helped me into the local hospital's casualty department before taking off again for London, in a panic because by now his delivery was late.

I waited for about an hour before a doctor saw me, but after hearing what had happened he said he couldn't help me – he didn't even examine me – because I was on the run. The sister in charge told me I should go to the police for help, which I did. I called them from the hospital and told them the whole story and they said to stay where I was and someone would come for me. A police car took me to the local police station and an hour and a half later, as I lay groaning and moaning in one of the cells, who should walk in but Mrs Crystal. I think it was the first time I'd ever been glad to see her. She took one look at me and loaded me into the back of her car. I think she could see I was past the stage where I could listen to lectures. She drove me straight to Newsham General Hospital in Liverpool, while I rolled about groaning on the back seat for the whole journey.

This time there was no delay. A doctor was waiting to examine me as soon as we arrived, but things by now had got out of hand. The pain was so bad that he couldn't even touch my belly without my screaming and there was no chance at all of his putting instruments inside me to see what was going on.

Once again I found myself being talked about over my head but this time, because of the pain, I couldn't have cared less. I was rolling about like a madwoman.

'I'm afraid she'll have to be admitted to hospital straight away,' I dimly heard the doctor's voice say. 'She has salpingitis.'

After that everything became a blur, the way it does in films when the heroine passes out – I don't think I quite passed out but my temperature was so high I suppose I must have been delirious and I hardly knew where I was. It was three days before I started to think straight again and a whole week before I was allowed out of bed, and I didn't even argue with them so I must have been pretty bad.

For the first week I had penicillin injections six times a day. They said the gonorrhoea had spread up my fallopian tubes and caused a serious infection inside me.

I was in hospital for six weeks altogether before they felt I was well enough to be discharged. The week I was due to leave Mrs Crystal came in one day with a big smile and the news that she had persuaded Mrs Roberts to take me back on condition I promised to behave and not run away again. I'd have promised anything to avoid returning to Falconer House, so the deal was struck there and then.

Everything was still the same at Elm Road North and after a couple of weeks it felt as though I had never been away. Not surprisingly I had lost my job at the hairdresser's, but Mrs Crystal got me a job as a nanny to a Jewish family who owned a nightclub as soon as I was well enough to work. I quite enjoyed that at first. I was looking after two boys of eight and eleven and they were good, but they had an older sister of 24 who didn't seem to like me; after six months I'd had enough of her criticizing me and I gave in my notice.

My next job was hairdressing again, but this time it was in Birmingham and Mrs Crystal arranged it so that I could live with Thelma because I was working so close to her, which was great. My boss was a Hungarian who called herself Lady Xaviera. She was really nice and we got on well together. In fact she used to say she would like to adopt me, though I was never sure if she was joking or not.

The trouble was that Mrs Crystal now had to tell all my employers that I had been in reform school, which meant that if ever anything went missing the finger of suspicion pointed straight at me. With Lady Xaviera it happened three weeks after I arrived there. A pair of her emerald ear-rings were taken from her dressing-table. Mrs Crystal broke the news to me and said I had been accused of the theft and would have to go back to Mrs Roberts' while the police decided whether to prosecute. They searched my things but of course they didn't find anything.

I protested and asked Mrs Crystal what she thought I could have done with a pair of emerald ear-rings. They wouldn't exactly have matched the sort of outfits I wore. I asked her if she thought I'd sold them to someone. She said that knowing me I had probably given them to a friend.

A couple of weeks later they discovered that it was the boyfriend of the daughter of the family who had stolen them and the charges against me were dropped. Although I got apologies all round I didn't feel like going back after that, so I was out of a job again.

While I was at Elm Road North this time I had got friendly with a girl called Vivienne, and together we decided to move out into a flat. Mrs Crystal agreed to this after a bit of argument, although she said she would still have to supervise us.

This was a breath of freedom and we both took full advantage of it. We found regular boyfriends and very soon they were spending half the night at the flat with us. I didn't sleep with them as an act of rebellion, and I certainly didn't do it because I liked sex. I discovered the first time it happened that I hated it. I couldn't ever get the memories of Uncle John and the black man in London out of my head when a boy was making love to me.

It sounds soft, but I think the real reason I slept with them was because each boyfriend had said that he loved me and I was so happy to be loved that I would have given anything in return, just out of gratitude, so sleeping with them didn't seem such a big deal. In the end each boy always found another girlfriend and we split up. I was sad for a bit but I wasn't heartbroken. In those last few months before I was eighteen I was thinking about something else which made boyfriends seem less important. I was approaching the end of my period in care. On the day I was eighteen they would no longer have control over me and I would be able to go back to Miranda.

It was a red-letter day, my eighteenth birthday. I can remember it clearly. It was like reaching the end of a gaol sentence. Mrs Crystal arrived in the morning and asked me what I wanted to do. I grinned at her.

'You can give me a lift to the East Lancs. Road,' I said.

I felt sorry for her in a way. I must have made her life difficult during the years she was responsible for me. She obviously felt she'd done all she could to help me, but it hadn't been enough. But the trouble with Mrs Crystal was that when I was growing up she was never able to get to know me – she just had to listen to what other people said about me ('Gloria's doing this' or 'Gloria said that') and she based her opinions about me on that. So I don't suppose she had much of an opinion of me because I'd never liked discipline and once I was in my teens I had never just sat down and accepted what people gave me. I knew I had my rights like everybody else and in the halfway house I was rebelling all the time at being treated as though I were a small child with no say in what happened to me.

I didn't think I'd had a fair deal. I'd been bounced around from one set of people to another, and all any of them ever wanted to do was get me off their hands. All I'd really longed for as a child was for someone to take me and listen to me and give me a bit of affection, which I'd never had. But I couldn't have told Mrs Crystal that. I think she'd have been embarrassed and so would

I, so I pretended to be hard, and maybe this was a mistake.

Anyway, Mrs Crystal did as I asked. After I'd said goodbye to Viv she drove me from the flat to the roundabout at the top of the East Lancs. Road and there she watched, looking a bit sad, as I unloaded my luggage from her car and walked up the slip road to start hitching to London. I'm sure she thought I was setting off to get into trouble again but she didn't say that, of course. She just said, 'Well, goodbye, Gloria. Good luck,' and drove slowly off in her estate car back towards Liverpool.

I was so excited. I knew Miranda would be waiting for me in London, although I hadn't written to her while I'd been in reform school. I'd hardly ever written a letter in my life. There hadn't really been anyone to write to and it just hadn't occurred to me to try to keep in touch with Miranda while I was in Liverpool. It would have felt unnatural for me in those days to sit down and try to talk to someone I knew on paper. But I was sure she'd be there in London still, and it would be as if I'd never been away. We'd just take up again where we'd left off, and I'd cook for her and she'd go on being an air hostess, and that would be my future. I wasn't looking any further ahead than that.

I got a lift to the outskirts of London and then caught a tube to Earl's Court. As I came out of the station and walked up the familiar road, my heart was doing somersaults and I started to run until I got to no. 19 and looked up at the attic window. Everything seemed exactly the same as the day I'd left and I pushed the doorbell excitedly, picturing Miranda's face when she saw me standing outside.

A strange girl answered the door. I couldn't believe it. She told me that Miranda had left the flat six months before and she had no idea where she had gone.

If I'd stopped to think, I suppose I could have contacted the airline and found her address that way, but I was thrown into confusion. With one lifeline gone, the only other one I could think of was Mrs Crystal so, feeling fed-up and depressed, I hitched back to Birkenhead and rang her home number. It was quite late at night by now but fortunately she was in.

107

She didn't seem surprised to hear from me – but at least she didn't say, 'I told you so', which was a relief. Instead she sat me in her front room and started ringing lots of different numbers and every so often she'd look up and say things like 'What are we going to do with you, Gloria?' and give a deep sigh.

I think it was then that I first got the feeling, which came over me more and more often in the next few months, of complete despair. I was a failure. It seemed to me as though I'd never be able to organize my own life. I always needed someone else to sort out the messes I got into. I felt hopeless, useless, worthless. For the first time I could remember I had a sense of really hating myself. I wanted to cry, but not in front of Mrs Crystal, so I just sat and stared at the floor while Mrs Crystal dialled on into the night, trying to sort out my life.

11

At about 11 o'clock Mrs Crystal finally managed to get hold of Vivienne on the telephone and asked her if I could move back into the flat with her. Vivienne agreed, so after a lot of discussion with people in the social services Mrs Crystal said I should do that until they got something else sorted out for me, and I moved back that night.

I don't know what the 'something else' was going to be and I never got a chance to find out, because before the authorities could do anything about moving me on other events had overtaken me and beaten them to it.

From the moment I moved back into Viv's flat things started to go wrong. I didn't have a job now and I couldn't generate any enthusiasm for looking for one. I went for one or two interviews but I knew from the moment I walked in that it was a waste of time. I felt no one would want to employ me after what I'd done, and I was right. Three weeks later I was still jobless and during the day I took to staying in bed rather than facing the question of what to do for the next nine hours while Viv was at work.

Something funny was happening inside my head. After staying in bed all day I couldn't sleep at night. I'd lie awake tossing and turning and crying my eyes out, though I didn't know what for. If Viv said anything a bit crossly to me – which she sometimes did, because often I didn't even bother to clean up the flat or prepare the supper while she was out – I'd burst into tears. I started to think about death all the time; thoughts of Nana and Gang-Gang were going round and round in my head. I felt I wanted to join them, wherever they were.

In the end I went to the doctor. I knew something was wrong with me and I was frightened. The doctor listened while I told him how I felt. Then he gave me a long lecture. He said everyone felt unhappy sometimes but it was silly at my age always to look on the black side. He told me I was young and had my whole life in front of me and I should look forward to it.

I caught the bus home to the flat. Vivienne was still at work. I went into the bathroom. This time, as well as Vim, there was a razor there which Vivienne had been using to shave her legs. I picked it up and started to stroke my wrists with it – gently at first, then harder. After the first line of blood appeared it seemed easy to make more. I changed hands and started on the other wrist. By the time I had finished there was blood everywhere.

I stared at it and suddenly the vivid colour of it against the white tiles of the bathroom seemed to bring me to my senses and I felt scared. I wasn't as sure as I had been that I really wanted to die but I felt tired – too tired to call for help. I lay down on the bathroom floor and went to sleep.

I don't remember my landlady knocking on the door to collect the rent or hearing her push the bathroom door open, but Viv said that that was how I was found in time so I suppose I owe her a lot. She called my doctor, who came and patched me up and got me to hospital. The next day I was transferred to Mostyn Nerve Hospital.

I stayed there for three-and-a-half months, having long talks with a psychiatrist and also ECT – electric shock treatment. I had four sessions. They said the treatment was to make me forget what had happened to me. I don't know which part I was supposed to forget. I hadn't told them everything that had happened to me, least of all what had happened with Uncle John. I couldn't bring myself to talk about that.

One day I was sitting in the ward doing some needlework, or occupational therapy as they called it, when a familiar voice said, 'Gloria. Is it you?'

It was Auntie Angela, the one who used to take me to gymkhanas when I was at the home. She had come to visit someone she knew at the hospital and had recognized me. She sat down next to me and held my hand.

'What are you doing in here, Gloria?' she said. 'You're only eighteen. You shouldn't be in here.'

I shrugged. 'The doctor seems to think I should be,' I said.

So she went to see the psychiatrist. I don't know what she told him but she was with him for an hour. When she came out of his office she came back to me and said, 'How would you like to come away to my house for the weekend? I'm married now.'

'What does the doctor say?' I asked doubtfully. I liked Auntie Angela but I felt safe where I was, as if I didn't want to move.

'He says you don't have to if you don't want to. It's up to you, but I'd like you to,' she said.

'OK,' I agreed, but without much enthusiasm. I wouldn't have admitted it, but I was scared and it was with my heart in my mouth that I set off to spend the night at Auntie Angela's.

During those first weeks at Mostyn I was on 250 mg a day of the tranquillizer Largactil as well as having the shock treatment, so maybe that had affected me, but whatever the reason I couldn't stand being away from the hospital. I stayed that one night at Auntie Angela's house, which was very nice, and I met her new husband, but I lay awake all night, convinced something terrible was about to happen to me, though I couldn't have said what.

In the morning I told Auntie Angela I wanted to go back and she didn't try to persuade me to stay. She seemed to understand, though she must have been disappointed. She took me back and told the staff at the hospital what had happened. She spent another hour with my doctor when we got back, and after she'd gone he sent for me to come into his office.

'The lady I've just been talking to tells me that she was one of your aunties from the children's home,' he said. I nodded.

'How was she to you when you were there?' he asked. 'Was she good to you?'

'She was the best one to me in there,' I said truthfully.

'She seems to think that the children's home is the cause of a lot of your problems,' he said.

What a genius! Where else did he think my troubles had come from when I'd spent practically all my life there? Six weeks of asking me questions and this had suddenly occurred to him? I felt like giving him a slow handclap.

He leaned forward in his chair and studied me closely as if to see what effect his next words would have.

'She seems to think that you were always pushed away when you asked for love,' he said. 'She seems to think that you always asked for it but you never got it. Would you say that was true?'

I looked at the floor. It made me uncomfortable to know that Auntie Angela had understood my feelings as well as that.

'I suppose so,' I muttered unwillingly.

The doctor sat back and smiled as though he'd just invented sliced bread.

'Good' he said. 'Maybe now we can work on something.'

So what did he do? Did he put his arms around me – did he organize it so someone could spend time with me and give me the love I'd missed? No. He made me draw pictures. Every day after that I had to sit down and draw pictures for him, after which he and the other staff would look at them and try to interpret them. If I drew a house and a garden they'd say, 'Ah, she wants to be married with a family of her own,' and if I drew a lion they'd say, 'Ah, that's all the anger she has buried inside her like a wild animal', when in fact it was probably because I'd been locked in a broom cupboard with the *Jungle Book*.

By the end of the time I was there I felt I would have made just as good a psychiatrist as any of them. I didn't rate them at all, but slowly – whether because of the passing of time or because of what they did to me, I don't know – I began to get better: at least, I got to the stage where I felt I could face living on my own again.

I was discharged from hospital one day in early August, having made up my mind to go back to London and try my luck again. Even if I couldn't find Miranda I felt I stood a better chance of finding my own feet down there where no one knew me than in Liverpool where my middle name seemed to be trouble.

So once more I set off thumbing down the East Lancs. Road. This time when I arrived I made my way to the West End. I'd read about the West End in newspapers. It was 1969 and London was full of hippies and flower people and squatters. The musical

Hair was sold out for months ahead – and the newspapers were full of stories about drug-taking and long-haired drop-outs and communes. Empty property was being invaded by crowds of young people with nowhere to live and the authorities didn't seem to be able to do anything about it. It all sounded incredibly exciting to me.

I arrived in London with no money and just a few clothes, in a suitcase which I dumped in a left-luggage locker as soon as I reached Piccadilly Circus tube station. Then I climbed up the steps and walked across to Eros, where the papers said it was all happening.

For the first hour I just wandered around watching all the tourists, who had also come to see where it was all happening. Then, when my legs got tired, I sat down on the steps of Eros. There were a lot of hippies sitting down there too, with long hair, kaftans, bells, the lot, and some of them came and sat down next to me and we started talking. They asked me where I'd come from, and they were so friendly and nice I felt I was one of them from the start. They asked if I had anywhere to sleep and when I said no they asked me to go back with them, which I happily did. I decided there and then I would become a hippy – for a while anyway.

That first night and for the next three weeks I slept in an art studio in a place called Broad Court near Bow Street police station. What I remember most about it was that it was freezing cold, even in August. They had these gas fires which I kept lit all night. I was told that I had joined a commune. They gave me a sleeping bag and everything I wanted. They didn't believe in individual possessions, and since I didn't own much and what I did own was safely stowed in Piccadilly's left-luggage lockers I thought the system had a lot to offer me.

The first night I was there I had a good sleep and the next morning two of the girls took me with them to Covent Garden. This, I learned, was part of the daily routine. We were given fruit and vegetables by the people working there – some of it a bit overripe or damaged, but still all right to eat.

Things were looking up. I said to myself, 'This is the life. This is for me,' and for a while it was.

I think the day I met the hippies was the start of one of the happiest times I've known and I think the reason was probably that I didn't have anyone telling me what to do. I was free to be who I wanted to be. It wasn't that I wanted to do anything terribly outrageous or crazy – I wasn't anxious to get into trouble with the authorities again – but the fact that there was no one standing behind me to check on me made me feel free as a bird, yet I knew I had friends who would help me out if I needed it. What more could I want? I asked myself.

I made friends with a girl called Kim and we used to go about together, exploring what for me was a whole new world. Our days soon developed a regular routine. I was fanatical about keeping clean. That was one of the things that put me off some of the others at the squat – they never seemed to think of washing and their hair and clothes always used to look dirty.

Kim was like me and always wanted a good wash when she got up in the morning, so we devised a plan. There was no hot water at the squat so when we woke up we'd get dressed and go down to the ladies' toilet in Piccadilly Circus. We'd pay the woman at the door threepence then go in and wash our hair in the wash-basin; then we'd strip off and wash ourselves all over and finally we'd dry ourselves under the hand-drying machine.

There was a big black woman in charge of the place and she soon got to know us. I can hear her worried voice now as she tried to persuade us to be sensible.

'Hello, girls,' she used to say in her strong West Indian accent. 'You coming in to wash yourselves again today? Oh, girls, you should find your way home, you know. This is not nice. You going to get sick coming down here every day standing about in the cold – and me, I'm going to get into trouble.'

She was a nice, jolly woman. We liked her. But she knew we weren't going to cause any problems. We'd just wash and then do our laundry and leave. Every day I washed out a bra and a pair of knickers and then we'd go back to the squat and hang them out to dry ready for the next day. Then we'd go up to Eros and tap tourists for money.

The things we'd do for money almost make me blush now. The best tourists were the Americans. They were so gullible. All the Americans wanted to see real London hippies, so that's what I turned into for those few weeks. Kim and I would dance around barefoot in the puddles, singing and smiling and being typical flower children.

One day I was dancing and singing on my own – I think Kim had gone to Covent Garden – and a middle-aged American couple came up to me.

'Oh, aren't you just cute, honey?' drawled the woman, at which I smiled sweetly and carried on dancing.

'Oh, Bob, you just have to get a picture of this girl,' she said. 'They're going to go crazy about her back home.'

My few 'proper' clothes were still in the left-luggage lockers at Piccadilly and since joining the squat I'd got myself kitted out with an old, threadbare black kaftan with tassels on the sleeves and hem that Kim had given me, together with some beads and bells which I'd bought from a shop in Carnaby Street, so I really looked the part. This woman couldn't take her eyes off my outfit.

'I just love your clothes,' she kept saying. 'Is this what hippies wear?'

'That's right,' I said, smiling and swaying as I pretended to be a flower blowing in the wind.

Suddenly she turned to her poor husband.

'I have just got to have them, Bob,' she said.

And she got them. They took me on a shopping spree to Oxford Street and let me pick a new outfit. I put my new things on in the changing rooms and the assistant wrapped my old clothes up and gave me the parcel, which I handed over to the American woman. 'Take them to America with my compliments,' I said. Then I took off my beads and cowbell and handed them over as well.

'The bell you can have on the house,' I said, grinning.

They hadn't finished with me, even then. After buying the clothes for me they took me out to lunch, and when we'd all finished eating they gave me £10 and waved me goodbye. I couldn't believe it, and neither could Kim when I told her.

So there we were with £10 between us – we shared all the money we were able to get together – and it was burning a hole in our pockets. We'd never seen that sort of money before since we started dancing at Eros. Neither of us were on social security, though I don't know why, because I suppose we were entitled to it, so £10 represented a real windfall.

The first thing we did was to go to the cinema that afternoon to see *Anne of a Thousand Days*, which had just been released, and when we came out, even after the ice creams and drinks, we still had about £5 left. We decided, after discussion, that this was our chance to find out what drugs were all about.

Nearly everyone in the squat took drugs of some sort, mainly grass or pot, and as a joint would get passed around most nights I'd had the experience of being high a few times. But I knew there were other things because I'd seen people taking pills and I'd been in the group when a pusher had come along and passed over tablets and powder in exchange for cash. Until now both Kim and I had been too poor and maybe a bit nervous of getting involved, but now we gave each other courage. We decided to go and sit in the coffee bar near Eros where we knew the pusher hung out. When he appeared we went over to him and asked for some Tuinal tablets, which everyone called 'sleepers'. I think it was 5 shillings for a 3-mg tablet, and we bought two each and took them with our coffee. Only you didn't say you took them, you said you 'dropped' them – if you wanted to be a part of the group it was important to get the language right. So we dropped them and then we walked to Eros and waited for something to happen.

What happened was that after a bit my legs didn't seem to want to hold me up any more and I fell over and lay on the ground and when I looked for Kim she was lying on the ground too, waving happily to me. We were both dragged back to the commune by the hippies. They really looked after you and I suppose that was the attraction for a lot of us – that it felt just like the caring family you'd never had when you were growing up.

We woke up the next day a bit groggy but quite pleased with ourselves and determined to try something else. Over the next few days we took most of the other soft drugs that were popular then: slimmers like Dexedrine and speed and blues, but nothing hard. For a start I didn't have the money, and also I had a terror of needles after my weeks in the hospital being injected with penicillin.

One night while we were down in Piccadilly I started talking to a bloke called George. George was the resident pusher in the squat. He didn't exactly blend into the background the way you imagine pushers would try to do to avoid the police. He used to wear a black top hat with a feather in it and he had a big blond beard and a long red soldier's coat, like the Beatles wore on the *Sergeant Pepper* album cover. He used to sell marijuana and acid to anyone who wanted it.

He seemed a nice guy, George, but he always looked serious, whereas I was always bouncing around chirping like a canary that had escaped from its cage, so we'd never had much to say to each other before. This night I went up to him.

'George,' I said, 'you and me have never had a talk, have we?'

'No,' he said, 'because you're always buzzing around. One minute you're here, the next you're over there. Sit down and calm down. What's the rush?'

So I sat down on the steps of Eros and started talking to him about the squat and drugs and comparing Tuinal with grass, me being the big drug expert by now.

Then he said, 'You've never taken acid, have you?'

'No, I've never had the money.'

'Well,' he said, 'I've got something for you. A present.'

'Oh yes, what?' I asked.

'You'll love it,' he promised. 'I'm going to turn you on to acid. I want to be the one to say that I did it.'

'OK, no problem,' I said.

I wasn't going to let him think I was scared. So what, I told myself, acid was only one step up from sleepers anyway. Little did I know. There, sitting on the steps, George gave me a full tab of purple haze. I learned later that it's better to trip with someone else and I also learned that most people start with half a tab, but now I just did what George told me and I dropped it there, sitting beside him. Then I wandered off, waiting for something to happen. Half an hour after I'd dropped it I went back to him.

'George, it's not working,' I complained.

'Don't worry. It will,' he said. 'Take another walk.'

So I went off again with Kim. We stood about and I was beginning to get fed-up and thinking I'd been given an aspirin as a joke when suddenly all the lights came zooming in at me and I was away. It felt as though my head was exploding.

I think purple haze was supposed to be the best acid you could get then. You got all the colours and everything and I was watching a firework display inside my brain.

It was getting to be night now and a bit chilly and I didn't have a coat on. I turned to George and said, 'I'm starting to feel all tingly.'

'Oh, you wait,' he said. 'You don't know what tingly means. You're only on the outside now. Wait till you get inside it.'

He was right. That night I learned what people meant when they said their minds had blown. I kept saying, 'George – look at all those colours, George.'

I was standing in the Circus by the cinema trying to tell everybody to look at the colours. They must have thought I was mad. I was up there for eight whole hours, and all the time George stood guard over me.

I used to go to a disco down the road from the Circus. It was always full of skinheads, but that didn't bother me. I thought that most of them were probably pretending to be skinheads the same way I was pretending to be a hippy. On this particular night, while I was still seeing stars, I went to the disco entrance and tried to talk to all the skinheads, but I couldn't because I was so high that I couldn't get the words out properly. They were all dancing and one came up to me with his hand over his mouth and started staring at me, so I stared back.

'What's wrong with her?' he said to his mate.

'She's tripping,' said his friend. He knew because your eyes go like saucers.

'So what! I'm tripping,' I said to the one with his hand over his mouth. 'What's wrong with you?'

'I've got toothache,' he said.

I burst out laughing. It seemed the funniest thing I'd ever heard.

'What's so funny?' he asked.

I couldn't move for laughing.

'You've got toothache,' I repeated, and collapsed. That's the last memory I have of that night.

Somehow I managed not to get locked up. Instead, George and some of the other hippies dragged me back to the squat at some time before it got light.

The next morning, back on earth, I found George and grabbed him.

'Oh, George,' I shook my head at him. 'What did you drop me?'

He laughed. 'Was it nice?' he asked.

I said, 'It blew my mind, George' – that was the way we really talked – and he started telling everyone else who was there what I'd done.

'What a girl! The first time she trips, she trips on her own and with a full tab too,' he said, and I started to feel quite proud. I decided to try it again, but when I learned that acid cost £1 a tab I soon changed my mind. I did trip two or three times after that but mostly I stuck to Tuinal, which was cheaper and not so scary.

I wasn't really worried about what drugs might do to me. Everyone I knew who took them seemed OK and I just didn't think about it. The only thing I refused to touch was heroin, but even that wasn't because I was worried about getting hooked. It was just my phobia of needles.

I remember hanging around Piccadilly tube station one morning and bumping into this guy we called Little Joe. He was pathetic. He was on crutches, but only because of heroin – injecting it into every vein he could find. He'd have injected himself in his ear if he couldn't find anywhere else. He was nice. I felt sorry for him. As I was sitting on the steps talking to him he took out his needle and put his arm over my arm. My stomach turned over.

'Oh don't, Joe,' I begged. 'Don't fix in front of me, Joe, please. Don't put a needle in your arm. Not when I'm looking. No, Joe, please.'

I was causing quite a scene and suddenly a copper came up and saw what was happening and called for his mates on his radio. He got hold of Joe's arm and was trying to pull the needle off him, then he turned to me and I recognized him as one of the coppers I'd met on duty outside the squat. I used to chat to them as we were going out and had got quite friendly with most of them.

'Gloria,' he said. 'What are you doing here? You don't belong here, girl. Go on. Off you go.'

'Oh, thank you,' I said gratefully, and with a guilty look at Joe, who had managed to put his needle in anyway and didn't seem to know what was happening, I cleared off. The coppers knew I wasn't on hard drugs and they were always all right with me.

Most of the girls in the squat had regular boyfriends that they slept with but for the first three weeks I was there Kim and I slept on our own and didn't bother with boys. Then, through hanging around so much on the Underground station at Piccadilly I got to know two of the buskers there who played the guitar and sang. One of them, whom everybody called Coventry Jack, became my boyfriend. He used to look a bit like the lead singer with the Small Faces pop group and I think I sometimes used to pretend to myself that that's who he was. I used to feel as though I were one of the Three Musketeers when I was with them. The other busker, Charlie, was a big black guy who used to wear a great wide belt like a weight-lifter. Not long after I met them they both moved into the squat.

As well as busking they used to work scams on tourists. They'd hang about in the lobbies of the big hotels looking for foreigners who wanted to buy cannabis, then sell them ground-up incense, which looked just the same. I used to go with them sometimes and it was after a few nights doing this that I started sleeping with Coventry Jack. He didn't ask me if I wanted to sleep with him. He just put his sleeping bag next to mine one night in the squat and I was too afraid of losing his friendship to say no. I still didn't like sex and I couldn't imagine that I ever would but if it kept men happy and liking me then I was prepared to put up with it.

My only real problem now was my lack of money. You could live on tourist handouts in London if all you did was hang about the commune smoking a bit of pot like some of the hippies did, but I had got a taste for the better things in life. I had hankerings for good meals in posh restaurants and trips to the West End cinemas and nice clothes, but by the time I'd bought some Tuinal tablets there was never enough left for any of these.

Then one day I was walking down to Eros through Soho, passing all the clubs with pictures of 'dancing girls' outside when I suddenly had an idea. I'd always liked dancing. Maybe this was the way I could get money for all these luxuries I was hankering after. Although I'd been such a late developer I had a pretty good figure by now with a big bust and the rest in proportion. Maybe I could dance about in a tasselled bikini some nights and get myself some pocket money. I thought it was worth a try, anyhow, and as it turned out I was right, although I had no idea then that I was at the beginning of a whole new career.

12

I never wasted much time once I'd decided to do something and that night when everyone was sitting around at the squat smoking and listening to one of the guys strumming on a guitar I plucked up my courage and slipped out to Soho. There was a club called the Moulin Rouge which I passed every day as I was going to Piccadilly. I made my way there now and asked the doorman at the top of the stairs if I could see the manager about a job.

He went downstairs, and a few seconds later came back up and told me to follow him. He led me into a little cubbyhole where a man dressed in a smart suit sat behind a desk. The man looked up as I walked in and asked what I wanted.

'I'm looking for a job dancing,' I said, trying to stop my voice shaking.

'You mean stripping,' he corrected me.

I shrugged. In for a penny, in for a pound, I thought.

'Yes, OK,' I agreed.

He looked me up and down as though I were a used car someone was trying to sell him when he already had a Rolls-Royce. When he'd finished looking he said, 'Have you done any before?' I decided honesty was the best policy.

'Are you kidding?' I said. 'I've never even been inside a strip club before. Are you trying to put the blinds on my character?'

The manager grinned. 'OK. You'd better get up on the stage and see what you can do,' he said.

He opened the door and led me out into the club. An act was already on and I could see a dark girl swaying under a spotlight looking bored as she removed her bra in time to a Shirley Bassey record. Around her in the darkness sat scattered figures staring silently up at the stage.

The manager looked at me. 'Well, how about it?'

'What, in front of all those men?' I asked, shocked. I'd thought I'd have a private audition or something first. I wasn't sure I was ready for this.

He laughed. 'Yes. In front of all these men. What do you think striptease is?'

'I don't know. What do I do? You'll have to tell me.' I could feel the panic rising.

'If I have to tell you then you can't do it,' he answered.

I gulped and thought again about it.

'I'll need a drink,' I said.

He gave me not one drink but three double brandies while I watched some of the girls do their acts.

After the second drink I decided there wasn't a lot to it after all. The girls came on stage with their clothes on. They took their clothes off more or less in time to the music, fluttered their eyelashes a bit and looked dead bored. The more brandy I drank the easier it looked.

After the third drink I went into the back behind the stage and a girl gave me a blue and white chiffon dress to put on. I'd put my best black bra and pants on before I set out. They asked me what record I wanted and I remember I picked Dionne Warwick singing 'Do You Know the Way to San José?' The girl put it on the record player and as the first notes played I took a deep breath and danced on to the stage.

The first thing I realized was that without my glasses and with the lights being so bright I couldn't see any people in the audience at all, so that was OK. It was one of my favourite records and oiled by the brandy I just started dancing and having a good time as though there really was no one else there. After a bit I started to take my dress off and everything was going great with all the brandy warming my insides. Knowing that people were sitting looking at me out there in the dark I started to feel really good, really important.

Then, just as I was wondering why I'd ever imagined striptease was difficult, disaster struck. The zip got trapped in the dress material when it was halfway down. Three times I tried to pull it loose. I was in a cold sweat. The one thing I dreaded was that someone would start to laugh at me. I couldn't have taken it.

I thought, 'They've done it on purpose to make me look stupid,' and the idea made me so mad that I gave one last yank at the zip. All at once the chiffon ripped loudly and down it came, while all the men started cheering. After that it was easy. The rest of the gear came off while the men carried on cheering and clapping until eventually I stood there as naked as a baby, just as the record ended and the lights went off. I couldn't believe it. The men were still cheering after I came off-stage.

I stood behind the curtain shaking and the stripper who'd lent me the dress came up to me.

'That was all right, girl,' she said with a smile. Then she saw me trembling. 'What's the matter?' she asked.

'Nothing,' I answered, shaking like a leaf. 'Only can I have another drink, please, before I fall over?'

That was it. The manager gave me £1.50 and said I had a job. He said he'd pay me 50 pence a spot, take it or leave it. I said I'd take it. The next night I went back and this time no drinks, nothing: I went straight on stage like a duck into water. I decided this was what I'd been born for.

Over the next three weeks I stripped maybe three or four nights a week and got better at it each time I danced. I enjoyed it and maybe this came across because the audience used to like me. After a bit the regulars got to know me and they'd shout, 'Gloria' before I came on.

Although I'd had a terror that people would laugh at me at first, once I got confident I started trying to make them laugh. I'd introduce bits of comedy into the dancing, like being very sexy one minute and the next minute pretending to trip over. Sometimes, remembering my first night, I'd act as though my zip were stuck again and pull faces as I pretended to yank it open. The audience loved it and I loved doing it. What I noticed and what I felt most was that when I took my clothes off everyone wanted to know me. I had everybody's attention. It was like giving a cat cream. When I was in the home I'd always been so plain. I never had a proper boyfriend until I left and no one had ever told me I was pretty. But suddenly, I got undressed and I was no. 1. No way was I going to stop. I decided that first week that if I couldn't be a lion-tamer, then I would make striptease my career. Over the next few weeks I found work in four other clubs in Soho and would flit from one to the other. As soon as I'd finished a spot in one club I'd pull my clothes on and run to the next, bras and knickers flying out of my bag as I ran along the pavement. Another quick show and it was on again until I was back in the first club ready for the second spot. I could do twenty or more spots in one night that way and at 50 pence a spot the money started adding up.

By now I'd been in the Bow Street squat for about six weeks and I was beginning to think about moving out and finding a flat as soon as I had made enough money from stripping.

Then, overnight, the squat was closed down. I don't remember exactly how it happened but I think somehow the bailiffs got in and we were locked out. We were all in a panic and there was a big meeting to decide where we were going to go next. There must have been about twenty of us. Fortunately someone said they'd heard there was a beautiful place in Piccadilly that had just been occupied, so we all picked up our sleeping bags and went in a procession to find it.

It turned out to be no. 144 Piccadilly, and whoever had told us about it was right. It was a beautiful place. It was next door to a house where the Queen used to live before her family moved to Buckingham Palace, and it seemed like a palace to me after six weeks in the studio.

I had no idea who the owner was or why it was empty. I just followed the crowd like a sheep, and when everyone else decided to stop there I did too. Three weeks of stripping hadn't given me the money to get the sort of flat I wanted and I decided squatting would suit me for a while yet.

The house was already pretty full when we moved in and it seemed to be quite different from and a lot more organized than the squat we had left. For a start there was a leader who kept everyone in order. We called him Dr John. The others said he was a professor, but later, when the papers started to write about the squat, they said his name was John Moffat and he wasn't really a doctor at all.

Kim and I ran through the whole building, yelling with delight like kids at what we found. Not only did it have running water, though granted it was only cold, but all the main electricity switches were connected. There were even elevators which worked. In the back garden there was a goldfish pond and from the top-floor windows you could look right out over Hyde Park. You wouldn't have got much more at the best hotel in London.

Dr John gave the rooms out in order of priority, depending on who'd been in the last squat the longest. He himself had taken the best room, being the professor.

Kim and I were given a nice room with a balcony, which suited us fine. In the morning we were able to do our laundry and hang our clothes over the balcony rail to dry.

I don't think we expected such a life of luxury to last for long. It always seemed too good to be true and sure enough it was. A few days after we moved in, the papers started to make a big thing out of the Piccadilly squat because it was in such a valuable property.

Because the mansion didn't have hot water Kim and I were still making our morning trip to the Piccadilly toilets for a wash and brush-up. Two days after we arrived at 144 we came out of the front door to be met by a crowd of reporters and photographers wanting to know what was going on inside.

We ignored their questions and walked off, but later I started to think about it and I realized that here was a chance to make some money.

'Get in there, girl,' I thought. 'They're always after stories.'

That afternoon the photographers started knocking on the door of 144 but the hippies wouldn't let them inside.

'No, we don't want any photographs,' they kept saying. 'They'll use them against us in court.'

I said, 'Hang on. Let's find out. Maybe it'll do us some good,' and I stuck my head out of the window.

'Which paper are you from?' I shouted down.

'*Sunday Mirror*,' one of them answered.

'OK. One minute, I'll be out,' I yelled.

'Don't worry,' I said to the others. 'I'll talk to them. I'm good like this.'

'Gloria, don't stir it up,' someone said.

'No problem. Leave it to me.' I had bags of confidence since I'd started dancing. I was a changed woman.

So out I went. As well as the *Sunday Mirror* there were reporters from *The Sunday Times* and the *Sunday Telegraph*. I think the *News of the World* was there as well and for some reason so was Reginald Bosanquet's brother – with a television news team. I was high on all the attention.

One of the TV teams wanted to push the flower children, peace and love thing so I found some flowers from somewhere and started handing them out. I gave the TV men a big bunch and told them to give them to Leonard Parkinson and tell him I thought he was sexy. I had a big crush on Leonard Parkinson that year, though I don't suppose I'd seen a TV for two months.

Over the next few days the reporters got to know me. I suppose they looked on me as their mole in the commune. They would take me to Charing Cross, where I'd beg a shilling off them so I could use the public baths there.

'Before you have an interview with me, I have to be clean,' I'd say snootily. Oh, I loved it. It was as if I were a film star, the way they followed me around.

Then, when I'd had my bath, I'd say to whichever reporter was paying for my story that day, 'Right, now where are we going for lunch?' and I'd get them to take me to a nice pub and I wouldn't say a word to them about the commune until I'd finished eating and had a drink. If they started asking questions before I was ready I'd put on a film-star face and say, 'Please, not while I'm eating. Do you want to give me indigestion?'

They must have felt like wringing my neck, but they were good sports. They knew it was all a big game to me and they played along with it.

Then, when I'd finished and was comfortably full of steak pie and salad, I'd sit back and say, 'Right, now what do you want to know?'

All they'd ask me about was what life was like in a commune. Everyone thought we spent every night jumping in and out of each other's sleeping bags, and they seemed disappointed when I said that we didn't. Coventry Jack had moved on by this time so I didn't even have *one* boyfriend to talk about, let alone the half dozen they expected.

When I saw what they wanted I started making things up about what was happening. I had to if I was going to keep getting paid for information. Everyday life in the commune was about as exciting as watching paint dry. People came in, slept and went out again. The reporters didn't want to hear that, so I gave them what they did want to know – stories of drugs and drinking and orgies – and they lapped it up.

'Come again tomorrow,' I'd say. 'Maybe I'll have something else to tell you. How much do I get for today?'

'Ten pounds,' they'd answer – that was the going rate. 'But don't deal with anyone else. We've got to write an exclusive story.'

'Certainly not,' I'd say. 'But you come to me, not one of the others or I'll take my story elsewhere.' Then they'd hand over the money and I'd add it to the pile stuffed in my pocket.

'Oh, you're lovely, thank you,' I'd say, and off I'd go.

The next day there'd be someone from another paper there calling out, 'Gloria, where are you?'

It was like one of those Whitehall farces where you keep trying to avoid letting the wrong people bump into each other.

'Please wait. I'll be down in one minute,' I'd call to the *Telegraph* reporter, knowing that somehow I had to get rid of the *Mirror* man on the first floor and the *Times* man in the basement without any of them twigging what I was doing.

'Who's that?' they'd say if they saw me talking to someone else.

'Oh, no one,' I'd lie. 'He just wanted to interview my girlfriend. Look, I'll meet you at Charing Cross station this afternoon.'

I met them all over London. That week everyone wanted to talk to Gloria. After the second day Dr John wouldn't let me do my interviews in the squat any more so I set up meeting-places around town. I was so busy I needed an appointments diary. I didn't go to work at the Moulin Rouge at all that week. I didn't need to. I made £300 in five days by giving 'exclusive' interviews before they got wise to me. By that time the story was almost finished anyway as far as the papers were concerned.

Because of all the press coverage everyone was interested in us. We even had a champagne breakfast one morning. We were woken up at 4 a.m. by shouting outside and we found some men putting up trestle tables. They covered them with white tablecloths and put candelabra on them. I don't know who set it up. I suppose it was a publicity stunt but we didn't mind, and we all knocked back champagne until the police came and put a stop to it.

During that week we pretended to have fights and arguments outside 144 because the photographers wanted us to, but the truth was that we were like one big happy family. There was hardly ever any violence in the communes I was in. I liked the hippies. They were great to me and they were very loving to each other, all of them – very caring.

Sometimes Kim and I would talk to Dr John and he'd tell us about his ideas. He wanted to make the mansion into a refuge for the homeless. It wasn't right, he said, that buildings should lie unused while people had to sleep in the streets. What he said made sense to me but the authorities didn't agree.

On the seventh day of the occupation they sent the police in. We had known they were coming because some of the police cadets we'd got friendly with had warned us the day before and told us to get out of the way before the trouble started. It was almost as though they were on our side, the way they tried to help us.

But after talking it over we all decided to stay. During the night someone found lots of cases of coloured plastic balls in the cellar of the house. God knows what they were doing there. They were croquet balls, one of the girls said. There must have been about two hundred cases of these balls, and when the police raid started all the hippies began throwing the balls at the policemen. It was like a coconut shy with all the policemen's helmets being knocked off.

But in the end the police got in and once they'd got the door open they started arresting everybody. Everybody, that is, except me. It was as though I were invisible to them. I couldn't believe it.

I stood in the middle of them all. 'It's me,' I said. 'Why are you ignoring me?'

I recognized one of the policemen and went up to him.

'What's all this?' I said. 'It's me. Gloria. I'm one of the hippies. Why don't you want me?'

'Oh, Gloria,' he said. 'Go away. Go on. Can't you see we're busy?' and he turned his back on me.

I followed him as he dragged one of the real hippies outside.

'What do you mean, you're busy?' I said indignantly. 'I was staying here for a week. How come you didn't arrest me?'

Then he got cross with me. 'Gloria, the game's over. Go on. Bugger off. Let us do our job.'

'Policemen aren't supposed to swear,' I said angrily. It was all I could think of to say. I was really upset, which was ridiculous really but I felt I was being treated like a child. They'd arrested nearly everyone else, as far as I could see – but when it came to me, I was told to go out and play.

I left 144 and walked down Piccadilly carrying my sleeping bag and feeling hurt and rejected. It seemed as though it was my fate never to be taken seriously. I sat down at Eros and wondered what to do next.

There were fewer hippies around than usual – not surprisingly – but I recognized a few who had been at the Bow Street squat with me and asked them where they were staying now.

They had all moved to different communes but they were full of talk about what was going on in a place called Endell Street.

'Tell me, tell me, tell me,' I said, all ears.

They said that a guy called Mick – 'Mad Mick', everyone called him – had taken over a school. He was with a crowd of Hell's Angels who had appointed themselves as the hippies' protectors. I remembered Mad Mick. He was one of the few hippies I hadn't liked, but some of the others at Eros said they were going there so I thought, 'Oh well, it's a bit of fun.'

I went with them down to Endell Street, which was near Covent Garden, and we found the school, all barricaded up. There were about five of us and we heaved each other up on to the roof and then crawled in through the windows, holding on to the legs of the person in front so we didn't fall and break our necks.

Inside it wasn't a bit like 144. Everyone was shouting and arguing with each other. Some of them said they were going to fight the police and others didn't want to. No one seemed to know what was going on. I climbed the stairs to the classrooms on the first floor and as I did so I heard a crashing noise and the sound of wood breaking. It seemed that the hippies were pulling down the barricades and giving themselves up. I couldn't have been in there more than half an hour.

'Hey, come on,' I protested. 'Aren't we going to fight?'

'No, there's too many of them,' they said. 'It's not worth it.'

'You mean I've nearly broken my neck climbing in here just for you to surrender?' I asked.

'Looks like it,' they said.

For once I was speechless.

The next minute the police burst in and this time it was for real. I was arrested. They were different policemen, not the ones I knew and was friendly with from sitting around Eros and 144. That was West End Central. These were Endell Street policemen.

It was a police sergeant who arrested me – a big chief. He said, 'Come on, let's go,' and we walked out of the door of the school. Then suddenly flashbulbs were going everywhere. All the reporters were there and I was recognized. A voice shouted, 'Gloria' and then others joined in.

'Don't talk to me – no stories, no pictures, not like this,' I said. I was suddenly ashamed and hid my face the way I'd seen people do on the news.

'Gloria, have you got a story?' said one of the voices.

'No,' I said, 'I've nothing to tell you.'

I got into a police van with some of the others. We were driven to the station and interviewed, one after the other. When it came to my turn the sergeant asked me what I had to say for myself.

I said I was hungry and I hadn't got any cigarettes and he wasn't so bad because he brought me a pack of cigarettes and two rounds of sandwiches. Maybe he thought that with my obvious press connections he'd better keep me happy.

We went to Clerkenwell Court the next morning and were told we were going to be remanded in custody for six weeks.

I came down to earth with a bump. 'Does that mean I'm going to prison?' I asked a policeman.

'That's right. Holloway,' he said cheerfully. Suddenly I felt sick and all the excitement drained out of me. I suppose I'd thought being arrested only meant being told off and let go again and now here I was in big trouble, it seemed.

All of the other girls were going to prison too so we chatted to each other and tried to cheer ourselves up.

We were taken to Holloway together in a police van. Before we were admitted we had to have a shower and then while we were undressed we had to bend over – so the warders could see if we had any drugs tucked away between our legs. 'Bloody hell,' I thought. 'I'm not that desperate.' Then we got dressed again – we were allowed to keep our own clothes because we were only on remand – and when we were ready we were shown to our cells and locked in.

The cells were horrible. I've seen a TV programme about Holloway since I was there and on the screen it didn't look too bad, but in real life it was awful. I slept in a cell on my own with a really hard bed – it was like sleeping on a board. Under the bed was a potty. Apart from that the room was bare. The worst thing was that half the window panes were smashed. I think they got broken so often the prison authorities didn't rush to replace them, so I nearly froze that first night.

In the morning a warder unlocked the door and I bolted out like a rabbit out of a hole. We were allowed to go and wash our clothes and have breakfast together in the dining room, though that was a grand word for it. It was filthy with crumbs and bits of food dried into the tiles on the floor. Then, after breakfast, it was back to the cell.

I tried to charm one of the warders into letting me stay out a bit longer, but my chat didn't work in here.

'Girl,' she said. 'This is not Butlin's. Back in there.'

I said, 'Oh, I don't like being locked up.' I felt like a little girl again. It was like being in the broom cupboard.

'You should have thought of that before, shouldn't you?' she said, pushing me back inside.

The days dragged. Once a day we were allowed out for a ten-minute walk around the parade ground. I remember one time I ran over the garden in the middle and a big warder chased me and shouted – I was terrified. They looked as though they could eat you for breakfast, some of those women.

On Sunday we were asked if we wanted to go to chapel. Nearly everyone said yes, just to get out of the cells. I wasn't confirmed or anything but when they asked if we wanted to take communion I thought, 'Why not?' So I did, and I drank as much wine as I could gulp while I held the chalice. The priest was wise to that, though. I don't suppose I was the first to have tried it and he grabbed the chalice back pretty smartly.

And then, just as I was starting to get really depressed, a miracle happened.

One morning, when I'd been in there about four days, a warder came and let me out of the cell. 'You've got a visitor,' she said.

I thought she'd made a mistake. I couldn't imagine who it would be. All my friends had been arrested too. I thought maybe it was Mrs Crystal. But it wasn't. I was shown into the visitors' block and told to sit down at a table – and there, sitting opposite me behind a grille, was Miranda.

'Hello, Gloria,' she said, and it was as though she'd only seen me yesterday. She had her boyfriend sitting with her. A new one.

She looked just the same, smart, pretty and kind. I felt as though I'd woken up from a bad dream.

'How did you find me?' I asked.

'It wasn't hard,' she said, smiling. 'You've been on television and in all the papers.'

'Well, I had to do something to get you in touch with me, didn't I?' I laughed. I was so happy to see her.

'Yes, but this is a bit extreme, Gloria.'

We were giggling and chatting away as though we were at a party, not in a prison. There was a warder standing in the corner listening to everything we said, but we just ignored her.

I told Miranda I'd tried to find her. She said she'd moved but she'd left a forwarding address at her old flat and the new people should have given it to me.

'Anyway,' she said, getting businesslike, 'I've left a carton of cigarettes downstairs for you and some sweets.' She knew I liked my sweets.

Then she leaned forward. 'We're going to get you out on bail,' she said.

I gasped, 'What – am I coming to stay with you?', hardly daring to believe it, and she said yes. Then she introduced me to her boyfriend, who hadn't said a word and looked gobstruck by the whole situation. Then they had to go.

It took four more days for them to get me bail, but thanks to Miranda's cigarettes I almost enjoyed the rest of that week. I didn't smoke very much but some of the other girls did and it didn't take long for the news to get round the grapevine that Gloria had two hundred cigarettes.

Because we were locked in for so long all the girls used to smash the windows of their cells so they could talk to people in other cells, and although mine had been mended I soon decided I'd rather be cold than isolated – so I'd broken them again. As it happened, that October the weather was really freezing at night, but Miranda's cigarettes proved to be my salvation. Every night after her visit the only conversation I heard through the window was 'Gloria – have you got a cigarette?'

'Yes,' I'd say. 'But it'll cost you. You'll have to give us your blanket.'

Then, in the morning, I'd get up as warm as toast after a night under three or four extra blankets that had been passed through the window and I'd join the line for breakfast. It wouldn't be long before I'd feel a tap on my shoulder.

'Gloria, give us a cigarette,' a voice would say.

'I'll give you two,' I'd answer.

'Ooh, will you?' the voice would respond, astonished at my generosity.

'Yes, but give us your sugar.'

We were only allowed one tablespoon of sugar a day, but that week I had one in every cup of tea, which with my sweet tooth was worth more to me than a cigarette any day.

I was in my element for the rest of that week and by the Saturday, when Miranda came for me, I was down to my last pack of cigarettes and must have put on a couple of pounds in weight.

Even so, a week in Holloway was enough to make me decide that the life there didn't suit me any more than life in a children's home had. And when Miranda came to collect me I breathed a sigh of relief. Prison was an experience I had no intention of repeating.

13

Miranda took me home to her new flat, which was in Radcliffe Square. She shared a house with four other people, but it was a big house so I was able to have my own room. There were three boys and three girls including me. Miranda had told her flatmates all about me but they didn't seem to mind that I'd been in prison and were quite friendly towards me. One of the conditions of my bail was that I had to sign on at 6 p.m. every night at the police station, and the people in the flat used to take it in turns to go with me.

Miranda let me wear her clothes again as I only had the clothes I stood up in at first, but even after I'd collected my suitcase from the left-luggage office at Piccadilly my worldly goods amounted to very little.

I was anxious to pay my way in the flat so that no one had an excuse to moan about me, and I started to look for a job. I knew now I could make £4 or £5 a night stripping and enjoy myself as well, so one day I borrowed some clothes and jewellery from Miranda and her girlfriend, dolled myself up and walked into a club in Mayfair to ask for work. To my disappointment they said they didn't need any strippers just then, but they were short of hostesses, if I was interested.

I knew all about hostess work from watching them in Soho. Basically all you did was chat to the customers, keep them happy and get them to buy you drinks and cigarettes at ridiculous prices. You only got paid about £5 a week as a straight wage but you worked on commission, so the more you got the customers to spend at the club the more you took home in your pocket. It seemed like money for old rope to me so I said I'd give it a try until a stripping job came up and I could get back to my 'real' career.

Miranda and her friend took me to Kensington Market to buy

some clothes suitable for a hostess to wear. We had a hilarious time choosing them. We all tried the gear on that night at the flat to see who could look the most outrageous and show the most cleavage. I said we should *all* go and work at the club, but they didn't seem so keen on that idea.

I started work the next night. The club was called the Blue Angel and was run by a married couple. The wife, Pat, was very beautiful and her husband Larry was very handsome and always immaculately dressed. To me they looked like a couple of film stars.

As clubs go, it was quite respectable and everything was run above board. Pat and Larry were very straight and fair with their girls and we got paid on the dot. I soon found out that some of the hostesses used to disappear with their clients after a few drinks and take them off to a hotel room somewhere, but if they did that it was a private arrangement and nothing to do with the club, so I never had any pressure put on me to sleep with the customers. I think I'd have left if I'd been asked to. I didn't think I'd ever be that hard up. The thought of sex still made me feel sick.

The nearest I came to doing 'business' was one evening when Pat asked me to go and sit with a regular customer who was a banker. She told me he liked to be teased so I stayed at the table all night and flirted with him, and he kept touching my leg and slipping me fivers. He gave me £15 altogether and that was that. I didn't have to go out with him or anything.

Most nights all I did was sit around, chat the men up and keep them happy. Although it started off as just a job, after a while I found I actually enjoyed it. I had always had the gift of the gab and all you had to do was persuade these men that they were the greatest. Most of them didn't take much persuading...

'Oh, you are nice,' I'd say with an adoring smile. 'You know, you're really very good-looking...Shall we have another bottle of champagne?'

You had to be prepared to lie through your teeth, because you got some real creeps in. All they wanted to do was talk about themselves and complain about their wives. Sometimes it was a job keeping my eyes open, what with being bored to death and drinking so much champagne.

It never struck me that there was anything wrong about what I was doing. The customers knew the deal, and if they were prepared to pay a lot of money to have a pretty girl spend the night chatting them up, then that was their choice.

One night two policemen came in. They remembered me from 144 Piccadilly and they said to Pat when they saw me, 'Boy, you do pick them, don't you?'

'What do you mean?' asked Pat suspiciously.

'I remember this one when she was a hippy,' said one of them, grinning at me.

I tried to shut them up before they said any more. I was still on bail and didn't want Pat to know about it as I thought she might sack me. But I wasn't quick enough and the whole story came out. Luckily for me it didn't bother Pat and Larry. If anything, it made them a bit more protective towards me and they started to take me to sign on at the police station. Being only eighteen years old, I was the youngest girl working at the club, and I think they felt a bit responsible for me. Sometimes, if I'd been working long past midnight and didn't want to disturb Miranda and the others by going in late at Radcliffe Square, Pat and Larry would take me home with them to their house in Harrow.

They had a beautiful house, very luxurious, and I had my own bedroom when I stayed there, all done out in pink. One of the things I liked best about it was that they had a lovely white alsatian called Baron, and after I'd been there a few times he was eating out of my hand. I always seemed to get on well with animals even though I'd never had pets of my own.

Larry had an Aston Martin and a Rolls-Royce and he would take me back to the house in one or other of them after work most nights. I'd sink down in the back seat, high on champagne, and practise waving royally to adoring crowds.

A funny thing happened once when I went to Harrow for a weekend. They had a sauna in their house. As I'd never been in one before I couldn't wait to try it. Pat said she'd take a sauna with me but someone telephoned her and she had to go out so I went in on my own. I had a shower first and wrapped myself in a towel as she'd told me to do, took my glasses off and went in.

Everything was a blur without my glasses and I groped my way round the little panelled room and sat down on a bench. It was so hot I could hardly breathe. Every time I took a breath the inside of my nose burned. I kept trying to get away from the coals which were giving out the heat so I was climbing higher and higher up the benches, only to find the heat was getting worse. Then I found I was sitting next to a bucket of water with a silver ladle in it and I breathed a sigh of relief. No one had told me the water was for pouring on the coals to cool them down, so what did I do? I drank the water. I drank just about the whole bucketful, scooping it up with the ladle. By the time I'd finished I was gasping for breath and I staggered out of the door thinking I was going to collapse. When Pat came home I told her I hadn't liked the sauna.

'Why do people enjoy doing that to themselves?' I asked her. 'I was so hot I thought I was going to die – and fancy making you drink water out of a bucket.'

She laughed herself silly.

I had been working in the Blue Angel for about three weeks when Pat came up to me one night when I was sitting in the bar at the club and whispered, 'Guess who's in tonight? John Bloom, the washing-machine king.'

Even *I* had heard of John Bloom. His name had been in all the papers recently. People talked about the John Bloom empire. He was sitting in the front row, and Pat told me he owned some clubs in the West End.

'We'll show him he doesn't have all the best dancers,' she winked at me. A few minutes later she came back with a guy in tow that I hadn't seen there before.

'I've got just the person for you, Gloria,' she said. 'You like dancing, don't you?'

I said yes, wondering what she was up to.

She introduced me to the fellow whose hand she was holding. I think she said his name was Gary. What she didn't tell me was that he was the dancing champion of Southern England. He held some dancing title anyway and he was very, very good, but I didn't know that yet. I was all dressed in white that night, I remember. It was just when 'dolly-bird' fashions were popular and I really looked the part. I had these nice new shoes on – soft, silver leather with my toe poking out – and a very short white mini-skirt, a white satin top revealing a bare midriff, and my hair was all done up in curls and backcombed. My figure was pretty good despite my sweet tooth – 36-24-36 I was then, and I weighed 9½ stone.

This dancing champion looked down at me and said, 'Can you do the jitterbug?'

Well, when you're sitting down and you've had a drink or two you think you can do anything, so I said, 'Yes – of course I can. It's great exercise.'

So up we went on to the stage and before I knew what was happening this guy was throwing me around everywhere – over his shoulder, between his legs – as though I were a rag doll. But he was so good and I was so relaxed after a few glasses of champagne that I was able to go with him and follow him. I was upside down and all over the place but we danced really well together except that I must have had this amazed expression on my face the whole time. I couldn't believe what was happening to me – it was like being on a fairground ride. Pat was backstage and when we came off she couldn't stop laughing.

'He's good, isn't he?' she said to me. 'You should have seen your face.'

I didn't think any more about it but the next night the phone rang in the club. Pat answered it and called me over, saying it was for me. It was John Bloom. He wanted to know if I'd like to go and work for him in his club. Pat pulled the phone off me when she realized what was going on.

'Now listen here, John,' she said angrily down the phone, 'this is my girl. You leave her alone. If you want to talk about business, you talk to me,' and she waved me away from the phone. I was walking on air for the rest of the day. People were actually competing to have me work for them. I must be good.

The end result was that I did go to work for John Bloom and I think Pat must have got some money out of it. I suppose really that's what she was up to all the time when she made me get up and do the jitterbug. Maybe she'd passed girls on to him before. I don't know. But it didn't really bother me that I was being bargained for. It was one more boost to my ego. And in any case I was getting bored with just being a hostess. I wanted a change.

I started work at the Crazy Horse Saloon in Baker Street the next week and almost straight away I was allowed to do a show, so I was back to what I liked doing best – stripping.

I started working on my act and thinking of new ideas. I still did comedy routines rather than the straight acts most of the other girls settled for. One of the records in the charts at the time was 'Indian Reservation' and I got myself a Red Indian costume and put together an act based on a sort of war-dance with this as my backing. I was getting better with every show and I knew it. The customers used to cheer me and this was music to my ears – like drugs, only ten times better – and after finishing the shows it used to take me almost as long to come back down to earth as after getting high on marijuana.

I'd been at John Bloom's about two weeks when the time came for me to go to court. I was still living at Miranda's house and she found me a lawyer. He was young and quite nice, though he sounded like one of the royal family when he talked.

He had a long interview with me the week before the case was heard.

'You do realize what'll happen to you and your friends at this court hearing, don't you?' he asked me.

I hadn't really thought about it too much. I said I thought I'd be fined.

'Yes, but the police are probably going to ask for you to be bound over to keep the peace for a couple of years for a certain amount of money,' he told me. 'How do you feel about that?'

I said, 'Will that mean I have to be good for two years or I go to prison?'

He nodded. 'That about sums it up.'

I didn't like the thought of that hanging over my head and I told him so.

'I want to be able to work with a free hand, and then if I *do* get into trouble, well, I can just start over again,' I explained. 'But it makes me nervous to think I've got to stay out of trouble. I have accidents if I'm nervous.'

The lawyer leaned back in his chair, looked at me thoughtfully and then said, 'Well, I suppose you can always go into the witness box.'

I thought of Perry Mason on the television.

'The witness box,' I repeated. 'That's where the prosecution rip you to pieces.'

'That's the place,' he agreed. 'Are you up to it? Being ripped to pieces is a bit uncomfortable.' He smiled. He was throwing down a challenge to me.

'Yes, but then they're not dealing with just anyone,' I said. 'They're dealing with me, Gloria Lovatt. I can do it. I shouldn't underestimate myself.'

He looked amused, which annoyed me, and I made up my mind.

'Anyway, at least I can try. I may as well go out with a fight as not do anything.'

So the lawyer agreed we were going to fight. He knew everything that had happened. I'd told him the whole story.

When the day came, everyone else who'd been barricaded in the school had their cases heard at the same time. No one else pleaded not guilty and they were all bound over for £100 to keep the peace for two years.

Then it was my turn. I went into the witness box and was sworn in. It was all very serious and dramatic, though I was a bit disappointed that no one was wearing a wig. I hadn't realized it was only a magistrates' court.

The lawyer who was prosecuting was quite old and very stern-looking. He glared at me as if he'd already made up his mind he wasn't going to believe a word I said to him.

'Were you at 144 Piccadilly?' he began, but before I could open my mouth my lawyer sprang up.

'Objection,' he said. 'The cases connected with 144 Piccadilly have already been heard by this court. This is a new case which has nothing to do with 144 Piccadilly. It is concerned with the occupation of Endell Street School.'

The chief magistrate said, 'Sustained.' It really was beginning to be like Perry Mason.

The prosecutor looked down at his notes, then turned again to me.

'Tell me,' he asked, 'are you a hippy?'

I said, 'What's a hippy? I moved around with them for a while, yes, but I wouldn't class myself as a hippy.'

By now of course my wardrobe consisted of mod gear, which was very smart and tidy, and I looked quite unlike the previous bunch who had been in the courtroom who had worn long skirts or kaftans with their hair down their backs and beads and bells round their necks. I'd moved on in the last six weeks, and I think my appearance helped me.

'Very well,' said the prosecutor. 'Were you residing at Endell Street School in Holborn?'

'No,' I said. That stopped him in his tracks. He looked again at his notes before carrying on.

'On the day in question, when the police raided the school, the police sergeant who arrested you said he found you on the premises. Are you saying that's not true?'

'Yes, he found me there,' I agreed. 'But I wasn't residing there. I had gone there earlier that morning to talk someone into coming out of the school. I wanted to persuade her it was stupid to stay.'

I widened my eyes and looked innocent. Years of pleading with Uncle John had helped me develop my acting.

'My friend' (I slowed my words down to show how sincere I was), 'my friend was on the first floor. She said she wouldn't go and when I came downstairs to leave they'd put the barricades up on the doors and I couldn't get out.'

'If that was the case,' said the prosecutor, sniffing, and obviously not believing a word I'd said, 'when the barricades came down why didn't you tell the policeman who arrested you what you've just told the court?'

I was beginning to enjoy myself. Dramatically I turned to the magistrates.

'Your honour,' I said to the one in the middle, 'I knew if I told the policeman the truth he wouldn't believe me. They were treating us as though we were all criminals. I thought my only chance was to wait until I came here and then people might listen and I might have a chance of someone believing me. The police were very angry that day. Do you think they'd have believed someone like me? They thought they'd caught me in the act. They'd never-have listened to me. I'd have been wasting my breath.'

I paused. I could see my lawyer looking at me. This was not quite what I'd told him. I was embroidering it all as I went along, but the funny thing was that I almost believed it as I said it.

'Miss Lovatt,' said the prosecutor, 'are you employed at the present time?' I think he had the idea of painting me as an unemployed layabout, but he was actually giving me my big chance.

'No. I'm not employed,' I answered. 'I have been looking for a job, but no one would give me a chance and I know the reason, too.'

One of the magistrates spoke this time. 'And why is that, Miss Lovatt?'

'Because, your honour, I like to think that I'm an honest person and every time I went to look for a job they'd ask me if I'd ever been in trouble and I'd have to tell them that I've been in prison for a week – because that's right, isn't it, your honour?'

The chief magistrate nodded.

'And so,' I continued, 'my name has been blackened.'

I knew I was coming close to overdoing it but I was enjoying the performance too much to stop.

'I think it's going to be very hard for me to ever get a job again now – and if I'm bound over as well I'll have no chance of ever making a decent life for myself – no one will want to employ someone who's been bound over. And all I was trying to do was to stop a friend getting into trouble.' I stopped talking.

I had almost convinced myself. My eyes felt full of tears.

There was a big conference. All the magistrates whispered to each other and I was allowed to sit down. After a while the chairman sat back in his chair and looked at me.

'Yes, Miss Lovatt,' he said, and then paused while my heart did somersaults. It seemed as though minutes went by before he cleared his throat and said, 'You are free to leave this court and I'm sorry if you feel any injustice has been done to you.'

I floated out of court on a cloud. Miranda was there patting me on the back. My lawyer pulled a funny face at me.

'You had me fooled,' he said. 'Is that really what happened?'

'Not quite,' I said, 'but it doesn't harm anyone.'

Outside I saw the police sergeant, the one who'd given me the sandwiches. He raised his eyebrows at me. I said, 'Don't worry. You can arrest someone else later. I'm free. Bye!' and I left.

'Boy,' I said to Miranda. 'Don't you think Perry Mason would have been proud of me? I cut that prosecution to ribbons, didn't I?'

We all went out to celebrate that night. I took the evening off from work and we had a great time. But it marked a new turning point in my life.

The next day I was in a bit of trouble for not turning up to work and I realized I was getting fed up with always having to be where someone else wanted me to be. I liked stripping still but I was restless. I wanted to try something else, but I wasn't sure what.

I decided to have a go at modelling. I was getting much more confident about my looks now. Six months in London had changed my personality completely. From thinking of myself as the ugly duckling I felt now that my body was my biggest asset. I knew men found it attractive and I knew they would pay to look at it. I reasoned that the more men who saw it, the more money I'd get, so I decided to go for the big time. The agent I tried was called Beno Wega. He was a Czechoslovakian photographer in Fleet Street who specialized in nudes for men's magazines: just ordinary pin-ups – I wasn't ready for hard porn or anything like that. One of the girls at the Crazy Horse told me about it. She said she'd earned some money doing it.

I walked into his office one morning. I didn't have an appointment. In the office there was a fat man sitting behind a big old desk piled with papers and photographs. He pointed to a chair and I sat down opposite him. He said, 'Well?'

'I want to be a photographic model,' I told him.

'You want to be a model?' He didn't look impressed. I nodded.

'You think it's easy,' he said. 'All the girls, they think it's easy. Well, it's not. It's difficult.' He spoke with a strong accent but I could understand that he didn't give much for my chances.

'OK,' I said.

He looked bored. 'All right. Let's see your breasts.'

I was taken aback. Although I took my clothes off on stage every night my audience was sitting in the dark yards away from the stage and I couldn't see them. To strip off in cold blood and broad daylight in front of one old man was a totally different thing.

But there was no backing out now. So I thought, 'Oh well,' took my glasses off and pulled off my jumper and bra.

He stood up and walked round me.

'Stand up,' he said, and I obeyed. It was really weird. He didn't touch me. He just walked round me and looked at me from all angles, nodding to himself as though he was a doctor and I was a patient with two interesting boils on my chest. Finally he walked back behind his desk and sat down.

'Very good,' he said in his funny accent. Something about me had obviously pleased him.

'Yes, I think you can be a model. Your nipples are perfect.'

'My nipples?' I repeated, thinking I'd misheard him. I hadn't known my nipples were anything special up to then.

He nodded, 'Yes, with all the girls lately who've been in here we have to put sugar and water on their nipples to make them stand out for the pictures, you know? But yours, they are – how can I put it?' He waved his hands about searching for the word. Now I understood what he meant.

'Automatic?' I suggested, and he nodded, with a hint of a smile.

Well, my automatic nipples earned me about £120 in the next two weeks, which was quite good pay in those days, but I soon decided that my career had taken another wrong turning. I didn't like it. Being photographed was boring. There was no audience to applaud me and I got cold and goose-pimply. As far as excitement and glamour went it was about on a par with folding wet sheets in the laundry in Liverpool.

I stopped modelling and went back to working at the Crazy Horse club, but as spring came I realized something was wrong. I was earning quite a lot of money now but I couldn't settle. I liked stripping, yet I didn't want to spend the rest of my life in John Bloom's club. I wanted new experiences, new challenges. All the happiness I'd felt when I first arrived in London seemed to have disappeared. I was beginning to feel trapped again.

And then, one day, I saw a poster on the Underground for Billy Smart's Circus announcing its arrival the following week at Clapham Common. As I read the details on the poster it was as though a little bell went off inside my head. Blow the careers master, I thought. I'd show him that Gloria always got what she wanted in the end.

That night I went home to Miranda and told her I was off to join the circus.

14

The next Tuesday morning I walked up to the big top on Clapham Common and asked for an interview. I was sent to see Gary Smart, one of Billy Smart's sons, who was about my age. When I told him that I'd always wanted to be a lion-tamer he laughed and obviously wasn't as impressed as I'd hoped, but he said they might have a job for me if I didn't mind hard work. He took me to see the big cats first of all, but he said it wasn't a job for young girls. When I saw the size of the tigers I didn't argue. It suddenly seemed a silly idea to me as well.

But then Gary said they were looking for girls to ride the elephants and if I'd settle for that then I could start working that week. I decided it was close enough to my childhood ambition to satisfy me and I said I'd take it.

I started the next day. The circus was only staying at Clapham for a few days so I had to get myself organized before they moved on. I told Miranda what my plans were and she ddidn't try to persuade me not to go, but wished me luck and told me to keep in touch. I said I would, and I meant it then, but I was still as bad at writing letters as I'd always been and so the day the circus left London turned out to be the last time I ever saw her.

I picked up my wages from the Crazy Horse and told them what I was going to do – and that was all there was to it. I had joined the circus.

There was one other girl, Sally, who joined at the same time as me, and that first week we got some instruction in how to ride elephants from Billy Smart, who was the trainer. I'd never even ridden a horse before but I didn't find it too difficult. After only a couple of days we were in the ring performing with the other girls. We were given costumes which were supposed to be glamorous and exotic, although we didn't think so.

We wore black curly wigs, a short, ragged, leopard-skin tunic tied over one shoulder and black fish-net tights. We had to buy these tights ourselves, which took quite a chunk out of our pay because they cost £3 a pair and although they were very thick they only lasted for about three performances. The elephants' skin was so rough and coarse that it rubbed great holes in them. Around our arms we wore tight bands of brass, so the final effect was a sort of cross between Tarzan's mate Jane and an Eastern slave girl.

I was given an elephant called Boomer to ride. She was the largest elephant and knew most tricks so I was the no. 1 rider. She used to rear up on her back legs while I held on to her headdress, then wave one leg around and be rewarded with a loaf of bread. She was beautiful and very gentle. I loved being close to such a huge animal, knowing that she could hurt me if she wanted but that she liked me enough not to.

There were five elephant girls and we all lived together in a big trailer. Sally and I got on all right but the other girls had been with the circus for about six months and thought they knew everything, so they hadn't much time for us. I felt in my element right from the start but I soon discovered what Gary Smart had meant by hard work. On a typical day when we weren't moving to a new town, we'd get up and practise in the morning, then we'd go back and clean the trailer before we did our shopping for the day. After lunch, when people started arriving for the afternoon performance, we'd dress up in red costumes and walk round selling ice creams, programmes and drinks until we were due to get changed for the elephant routine and afterwards we'd have a quick break before we did it all again for the evening performance.

After the second show we'd all go for drinks to the nearest pub, wherever we happened to be. In general most people in the show kept to their own groups, so you'd get a little party of clowns at one end of the bar and a family of trapeze artists at the other, and in the middle, being ignored by both groups, would be the elephant girls.

It was fun, though. I got to work with a lot of animals and even achieved my ambition of getting close to a lion, though the reality didn't quite reflect my dreams. I was playing with a 6-month-old lion cub when it decided it wanted the choc ice I had been eating. I let it have a bit and then took it away, which I suppose was a bit like trying to take a bone off a dog – not to be recommended. The cub pawed my arm for some more and I still have the scar where its claw went in.

That year I did more travelling than I'd ever done in my life before. Soon after I joined the circus in London we moved on to Brighton and towns along the South Coast, then, a couple of months later, we travelled north to Leeds and gave shows at most of the big northern cities, including my old stamping grounds of Liverpool, Birmingham and Chester. Altogether I travelled with them for six months before the circus closed down for its winter break.

Like all the other girls I started to look for a job for the winter but I only wanted something to fill in. I felt the circus was in my blood now and I intended to go back for a second season in the New Year. It was the travelling as much as the animals which appealed to me. I wanted to see more of the English countryside and the towns which until now had just been names on a map as far as I was concerned. But Fate had other plans for me.

I decided to go back to Liverpool for the winter, with the idea of getting work in the clubs there. I had quite a bit of money stashed away by now, enough to get myself a flat, and once I'd found somewhere to live I talked myself into a hostess job in a small nightclub. The owner was called Norman. He was quite nice, about 40 years old, and I regarded him rather as a father figure, I suppose. He always asked how I was and made sure I had transport to get home after work. I liked being looked after. It made a change from always having to look out for myself.

But it turned out that Norman didn't quite see me as a daughter. On New Year's Eve he invited me to his house for a few drinks to welcome in 1971. I didn't have a party to go to and I felt a bit sorry for him as he was obviously going to spend the evening on his own if I didn't go, so I said yes. He lived by himself in Formby. I got very drunk, and after we'd both had a laugh over our New Year's resolutions Norman and I went to bed together. I don't remember very much about it, except for thinking that it wouldn't be very polite to say no after he'd been so kind to me.

I hadn't slept with anyone the whole time I was at the circus. In fact I'd only slept with four people in my life, not counting the times I was raped. I'd never done it because I was swept away with desire or anything romantic like that. Each time the only reason I'd done it was because I'd wanted to please people and this seemed to be what pleased men best.

I'd never bothered about contraception or thought about going on the pill – it's hard to say why. Maybe it was because I never set out for the night intending to end up in bed with anyone. It always seemed like an unpredictable accident when it happened. And I never believed it would happen again.

It was after sleeping with Norman that my luck finally ran out, and six weeks into the New Year I realized that I was pregnant. I was nineteen.

I didn't know what to do. I didn't think of telling Norman. I'd only slept with him once and doubted he'd remember much more about it than I did. Besides, I'd left his club by now and was working at a new one on the other side of town.

In the end, in desperation, I rang Mrs Crystal. She was quite good. She didn't seem surprised to hear from me. I suppose I was only living up to her expectations. She said she would try to get me an abortion. But I wasn't sure that was what I wanted. I wanted to talk about it to someone. My uncertainty must have been showing, because I saw three doctors before they could decide that I should have an abortion. Each time I thought I was going to get it over with I kept getting referred to another doctor and then the other doctor would be away on holiday or for some other reason wouldn't be able to see me straight away. By the time I saw the last doctor I was already fifteen weeks pregnant and they decided it was too late anyway. Brilliant!

I think now that if I'd had a chance to talk it through properly with someone and to understand what having a baby really meant and what choices were open to me I would have preferred to have an abortion. It would probably have been best for me but the decision didn't seem to be up to me. It all seemed to be taken out of my hands. It was as though I was back in the children's home again. My welfare officer took charge and I did as I was told without even arguing.

Although in London I had felt as though I had grown up very quickly, now that I was in trouble I was like a child again inside. I felt like a different person from the girl who six months before had been lapping up the applause in the big top.

Once the doctors had decided there was no chance of an abortion Mrs Crystal found me a place in a mother-and-baby home in Warrington. I left the nightclub where I was working and moved into the home when I was four months pregnant.

It was a strange time, that summer I spent in Warrington waiting for the baby to arrive. I started making white bunny rabbits and matinée jackets for the bump that was growing in front of me, but it felt unreal. I couldn't think of it as a real baby. It was just my big belly – something which burst the zips of my trousers and made it uncomfortable when I turned over in bed at night.

So I had no strong feelings before the baby was born about what I wanted to do afterwards and I didn't object when the authorities suggested adoption, although to say they 'suggested' it is an understatement. Everyone who spoke to me seemed to assume that that was what I was going to do. I don't remember the possibility of my keeping the baby ever being mentioned. Mrs Crystal told me about a nice couple they had found who wanted my baby because they couldn't have any of their own. She said they would be able to give it a good home because the husband was a bank manager and they had plenty of money, so I was very lucky...

And because I never realized that I had any choice I soon started to think about it as their baby. I didn't know that I had any rights in the matter. Everyone else in the home was having their baby adopted as well, so it didn't seem possible to consider another choice. It all fitted in with the reward-and-punishment pattern of my life so far. I'd been a naughty girl and was obviously unfit to be a mother so my baby would be taken from me and given to someone who was fit.

But I can't pretend I felt bad about it while I was pregnant because before the baby was born it was like talking about an imaginary doll, and I have to admit I was far more concerned about the dangers of the birth itself than about the child I was going to produce.

There were about ten of us in the home and at night after we were in bed we used to frighten each other silly with horror stories of nightmare labours and deaths in childbirth. All we seemed to talk about was how much it would hurt and how long it would last and whether you would have to be cut. At times I thought I probably wasn't even going to survive the birth, let alone have a baby at the end of it to worry about.

Some of the girls had been in before. One, called Sarah, had been in three times and was now having her fourth, so she knew exactly what was going to happen and took great delight in telling us all the gruesome details of her last three labours.

Getting stretch marks was the other thing that everyone worried about. I always used to put baby oil in the bath to try to prevent them. I thought whatever else happened that was the one thing that would finish me, because I'd never be able to strip again with stretch marks across my belly.

I nearly caused half a dozen miscarriages through my obsession. I'd pour all this baby oil into the bath and wallow in it for half an hour, but then, when I'd finished, I'd forget to put the rubber bath-mat back on the bottom of the bath. Later in the evening I'd be downstairs, there'd be a crash from the bathroom and a voice would scream down, 'Gloria, I'm going to kill you when I get out' — someone else would have skidded head-over-heels as they stepped into the oily bath I'd used.

One of the domestic helps at the home told me that if you do a lot of exercise it makes the birth easier. She was a bit sharp, that domestic, because she got me to do all the shopping – and I never argued because I was so petrified of the birth and so anxious to do anything that might make it less painful. The home was a big semi-detached house, half-way up quite a steep hill, and I used to come up this hill sweating and panting, carrying a case of tins under one arm and a huge bag of shopping over the other. When I wasn't shopping I used to run up the stairs two at a time and I'd jump up and dance whenever there was any pop music on the radio. I was fanatical about exercise. Sarah, who told me it was a waste of time, said she got exhausted just watching me.

The other thing which we all did was relaxation exercises. We would go down to the clinic every Thursday morning and lie about on pillows breathing deeply and practising going all floppy.

One Thursday, when the baby was just about due, I didn't feel like going to class. I felt strange. I didn't want to go out. I just wanted to stay in my room. It was a feeling I'd only ever experienced once before, when I was ill in the nerve hospital. After I'd got better I'd never liked staying in, so I knew this feeling meant something was happening. They made me go to the relaxation class anyway, and then at 10.30 that night my labour pains started coming, gently at first, like slight backache.

They took me into the cottage hospital, which was small and friendly, and they put me to bed. I already knew the staff there quite well because I'd been in there more than most of the other girls in the last weeks of my pregnancy. They'd discovered I was rhesus negative, and that meant they had to take my blood quite often. When I asked why, they said that if I ever got pregnant again I could have a blue baby unless they did all the tests. I was still terrified of needles and I used to try to kid them they'd taken my blood the week before, but they never fell for it. 'Gloria, you mustn't do that,' they'd say crossly when they'd looked up the records and found I was lying. I'd grin, shrug and say, 'No harm in trying.'

The night I went into labour there was a big black sister on duty. She was great. She had a real sense of humour – which she needed, because we nearly started off with a disaster.

The trouble happened because I didn't know what an enema was. There was a plummy-voiced physiotherapist who used to take our relaxation classes and one Thursday she'd said, 'When you go into labour, you'll be shaved and given an enema,' as though we all ought to know what that was. I didn't like to ask in case I looked silly but when I went into labour I wished I had.

All I knew was that the nurse stuck this big tube up my backside and I heard this sucking noise. She said the enema would 'clean me out', so I assumed that what she was doing was suctioning everything out of me like a vacuum cleaner. That's what it felt like, and you can't see behind you to see what they're doing to you so I never realized she was pumping stuff into me. At the classes they'd said the enema makes the baby's head come down easier, but they hadn't said how.

So I was still lying on the bed wondering how it was possible that I desperately wanted to go to the toilet when I'd just had a vacuum cleaner attached to my insides when the sister came back in.

'You still here?' she asked, as though she couldn't believe her eyes. 'Get going,' she bawled at me. 'You better move *now* if you are going to get to the toilet in time.'

I didn't need telling twice. I moved like a rocket and just made it. Afterwards when I came back and told the sister why I hadn't gone straight away she couldn't stop laughing.

I'd known all along I wouldn't have an easy time and I was right. It was a back labour, which meant that even when the contraction stopped the pain in my back didn't go away. I didn't want to be brave. None of that natural childbirth stuff for me: I took every drug I was offered and then demanded more. Over the next 24 hours I had three pethidine injections and then they gave me two syringes full of something they called a morphine cocktail. The black sister was on night duty and went off the next morning, but when she came back on duty I was still in the same bed, drugged up to the eyeballs but no nearer to producing a baby.

In the end the sister said, 'That's it – no more.' God knows why, but none of it seemed to have any effect on me anyway. Maybe it was because I'd been on sleepers and acid in London and had built up a resistance to drugs, I don't know, but if this was labour *with* painkillers then I decided I wouldn't like to try it without.

'Please, nurse,' I remember begging, 'please can I have another one?'

'Gloria,' said the black sister, 'we've given you enough to knock out a horse – you can't have no more, girl. You have to work later.'

Back labour – they say it's the worst. I couldn't lie on my stomach. I couldn't lie on my back. I couldn't lie on my side. I didn't know what to do. Then, some time in the early hours of Saturday morning, just when I'd convinced myself that I was going to die, the sister gave me the gas and air mask and for the first time things seemed to get a bit better – the pain was sort of blurred. I held on to the mask so hard she had to prise my fingers off it to get it away from me.

'That's enough for now,' she said. 'No more gas and air. Now you must work.'

Then she went out. She was looking after another girl in labour in the next room at the same time as me. The minute the door closed I grabbed the mask back and began huffing and puffing into it. But this time nothing happened. The magic stopped working and the pains came back into focus. I started groaning. The sister came back in and I threw the mask at her. 'You can take that away. It's empty,' I said. 'It doesn't work.'

She took one look and laughed. 'That's oxygen,' she said. 'You won't get nothing off that, girl.' So for twenty minutes I'd been trying to pant oxygen. 'God,' I said, 'never mind – the kid'll be intelligent anyway.'

It seemed like years and years later when all at once I felt a strange pushing sensation inside me, a bit like wanting to go to the toilet. After my fright with the enema I wasn't going to take another chance on messing the bed. The nurse was in with the other girl and I couldn't ask her what to do, so off I trotted to the loo.

Five minutes later, I was sitting on the toilet, not having any luck, when the midwife's voice floated over the top of the cubicle.

'Where's that woman now? Where she go?'

I said, 'I'm in the toilet.'

'Get off the toilet,' she screamed. 'You want to drown your baby?'

'I want to go,' I yelled back. 'I'll mess the bed.'

She burst into the cubicle. 'Will you listen to what I'm telling you, woman?' she cried, dragging me off the toilet and almost carrying me back to my room.

Suddenly I felt so tired I could hardly keep my eyes open. I climbed on to the high bed, turned over on to my side and put my head under the pillow.

'Turn over on your back,' she said. 'I have to examine you.'

'Oh, you won't give me no peace,' I grumbled.

She felt between my legs. 'Right now, the baby is coming,' she said. 'It's time for you to work.'

Everything was going blurred in front of my eyes – it seemed as though all the drugs were suddenly working at once. I rolled over on my side again and closed my eyes.

'What are you doing now, Gloria?' she asked.

'I want to go to sleep,' I said. 'Wake me when it's over.'

She pulled me over to her and propped me up, tutting and clucking all the while like a big black mother hen.

'Now, Gloria, this baby is coming. It's too late to sleep now, girl. You should have slept before. Now you must work, Gloria. You've got to push.'

She was a lovely woman. She stayed with me, holding my hand, making me push, cheering me on and somehow, in spite of me, my body started to push on its own. It felt as though I were being swept along in a whirlpool, with everything out of control. Then at last, just when I thought I was going to split in two, I felt something like a warm, wet fish slithering out of me down between my legs – and at the same moment all the pain stopped. I'll never forget that feeling. The sister held the baby up for me to see and I saw it all as though it was a dream in slow motion. 'A little girl,' I heard her say, and then I went to sleep. It was 7.15 on Saturday morning.

I slept for two days, waking only when they shook me awake to feed the baby. It seemed as though once I didn't need them, all the drugs finally decided to work.

On the third day I woke up to find that I had a daughter who weighed 7 pounds 2 ounces and was 21 inches long. I called her Coralie Jane.

I have to admit that at first I treated her just like a doll. For the first few days it was as if I couldn't believe this little thing had anything to do with me. I think I was more interested in the television than the baby that first week. All the mothers used to sit in the ward together at feeding time and we would treat feeding like a race.

'Come on, girl, come on, get it down you,' I'd say. 'I want to watch a programme in ten minutes,' and she'd suck away like mad. She was a good little feeder and we'd always be first to finish.

'Good girl,' I'd say. 'You're a winner, just like your mum. Now, back to bed,' and I'd put her down and rush away to watch whatever was on the box. It was like a game to me.

All the babies in our ward were being bottle-fed. No one suggested breast-feeding to me. I suppose it would have made it more difficult for me to pass the baby on to someone else, so they didn't encourage it.

Then, after nine days, I came home with Coralie Jane to Warrington and my feelings towards her started to change. I had to keep her for another week before I could sign the adoption forms and by the end of that week she was beginning to have an effect on me.

I was moved from the dormitory into the nursery to sleep, so the other girls wouldn't be disturbed when I had to feed her in the night. There was no one else with a baby in the home that week, so for those seven days Coralie and I lived together all the time, shut away in a little world of our own. I had a kettle and everything I wanted in there so I could make her feeds and my coffee. I didn't need anyone else for anything. It was nice, that week.

One funny thing I noticed was that I'd been a really heavy sleeper before I had the baby, but in the nursery I used to wake up automatically when her feed was due, before she cried or anything. I couldn't believe it. Six o'clock in the morning and *me* awake!

I'd look in the cot and Coralie Jane would already have her eyes open. She was a good little baby – she hardly cried at all. I'd make her a bottle while she gurgled at me and now that I'd left the hospital it wasn't a race to get her fed. I was enjoying it. She wasn't a doll to me any more.

They had a routine at the home for when the day came to give away your baby. They had this elderly couple – I don't know if they were paid for what they did or if they volunteered – and on the day the foster parents were due this couple would turn up and take the girl out for lunch at their house. Then, when she came back, the baby would be gone. This routine was supposed to make it easier for the mother.

So when Coralie Jane was two-and-a-half weeks old the time came and it was my turn.

I was a bit nervous. I was close to her now, but it had to be done: everyone said so. So I kissed Coralie goodbye and went out with these two old people. I sat at the dining-table at their house, feeling sick and trying to pick at my lunch. Suddenly the phone went.

It was the matron from the mother-and-baby home wanting to speak to me. 'Gloria, you must come back to the home now,' she said urgently.

'Why?' I said, instantly terrified that Coralie had been taken ill or died.

'A purse has been stolen and the police want to speak to you.'

I couldn't believe it. History was repeating itself. Something had gone missing so they were sending for Gloria. They had certainly chosen their moment well.

So I went back, and of course by the time I'd arrived they'd found the purse down the back of a chair and the police had gone.

But no one suggested I went back to finish my lunch, even though Coralie was still at the home. I went into the nursery and she was crying for *her* lunch, so I fed her, put her down to sleep and then went into the television lounge. Ten minutes later the foster parents arrived to collect her. I heard the doorbell ring, and the next minute the matron put her head round the door of the lounge. 'Gloria,' she said, 'they're here. Will you go up and get the baby for us, please?'

I hadn't cried since I left the nerve hospital in Mostyn, but I came close to it then. I was beside myself with rage and unhappiness.

I said, 'I can't go up and get the baby. You're mad! I can't hand my baby over to these strangers.' Matron hesitated and then shut the door and I heard her going upstairs to fetch the baby herself. A few minutes later there was the sound of the front door being opened and closed, and when I came out Coralie Jane had gone.

It took me weeks after that to start acting normally again. I think I went a little bit crazy. I'd go and make up bottles for her in the nursery and go in to check she was all right. I kept bursting into tears and making mistakes whenever I tried to do anything. They told me it was post-natal depression, which was quite normal and I would soon get over it. Mrs Crystal came to see me and asked me to give some of my social security money to her each week to pass on to the foster parents for the baby's maintenance until she was adopted. She said I could go and see her if I did that, but I said no, I wouldn't. I told her, 'I'll sign papers. I'll do everything you want me to, but I don't want to keep being reminded about her. I want to forget.'

I said I didn't want to maintain any contact because there was no point – they weren't going to let me have a go at looking after her anyway, so I felt I'd rather make a clean break from her.

I asked Mrs Crystal once why I couldn't have tried looking after her and she told me that because of my background I wouldn't have been a good mother.

Maybe she was right, but I know one thing – I would have

loved her. I knew how much I missed love myself, so that's one thing I would have made sure she had, and maybe having a child of my own would have given my life some purpose and settled me down. I still think about her. She'll be almost grown-up now, and if the bank manager *did* adopt her, as they said, then I suppose she'll have had a better life than I could have made for her – so maybe it was all for the best.

But no one could have given her more love than I had to give her. I'm sure of that.

15

They let me leave the mother-and-baby home six weeks after Coralie Jane was born. The doctor gave me a post-natal examination and said all my insides were back to normal and thanks to the gallons of baby oil I hardly had a stretch mark to show that I had ever been pregnant.

The day I walked away from the home for the last time I came to a decision. Thinking about my baby only made me unhappy, so I made up my mind that I'd try not to think of her again. I would pretend the last year had never happened. Strangely enough, I found that once I'd left the people who'd been around me when I was pregnant and the atmosphere of babies and motherhood, it wasn't nearly as hard as I'd thought it would be. It was as though a door had closed in my mind.

I decided I wanted to go back to stripping. Having got the passion for jungle animals out of my system I realized the one thing I still craved was applause – applause for me, not for an elephant I was sitting on. I wanted to be no. 1 again. I wanted the boost to my ego that came when people paid money to see me perform.

But I didn't feel like going back to London. There were clubs in Liverpool and what family I had was still there, so I got in touch with my sister Joyce and asked if I could stay with her for a bit while I looked for a job. Joyce knew about the baby and had been to see me at the home while I was pregnant. I moved in to her house in November 1971.

The same month I found myself a job in a Liverpool club called the Glad-Ray and started dancing. I didn't think of it now as being just stripping – there was more to it than that, and I knew now that my dancing was pretty good. I was to stay at the Glad-Ray for the next two years.

I had started working this time with the confidence that I knew what I was doing and it must have showed. My act soon became quite well-known. After I'd been there about six' months one of the regulars told me a story of how he'd been down in Southampton and had mentioned to a bloke in a pub that he came from Liverpool and this bloke had said to him, 'Do you know a club called the Glad-Ray and have you seen a stripper called Gloria?' Even down there they knew me. Hearing that story made me feel great. My fame had spread. It might not have been film-star fame, but it was the nearest I was going to get to it.

After a couple of months I got myself an agent and I started working in several other clubs on the Liverpool circuit. It meant long hours, but I didn't mind. Dancing didn't seem like work to me because I enjoyed it so much.

I think the reason that people thought I was a good stripper was that I didn't take it too seriously. I didn't try to look bored and sexy like some of the other girls did. I had discovered when I was dancing in London that certain things made people laugh and that people were more relaxed and enjoyed themselves more when they laughed. A bit of slapstick usually went down well and the men always liked it if you picked on someone in the audience and made a play for him. I developed my Red Indian act along those lines. I bought myself a new squaw's outfit and changed my war dance so that it ended with my pretending to scalp one of the customers. We had to buy our own costumes and most of my days off were spent hunting through the market for new ideas for these.

One thing I did that was fairly easy to dress for was a schoolgirl act, in which I'd carry a hockey stick and a satchel and look naughty and cute. Hidden in my satchel I'd have a water pistol, and half-way through the act when I'd got them all leaning forward in their seats I'd pull out my water-pistol and get some of the front row guys with it. But that one misfired on me. I was dancing in a club called the Asp one night where the club manager was a bit of a comedian himself: before I came out on stage he'd given every bloke in the audience a water-pistol and they started firing them at me. I was soaked, but I still had my wits about me.

'Right,' I said. 'Drop your weapons else I'm not taking nothing else off.' That stopped them.

In another act I used to dress up as a Gestapo officer with a riding crop. I'd got the uniform from an Oxfam shop. It wasn't a proper riding whip. It only had string on the end but I'd tie a knot in the string and whip the fellows in the front row with it while I shouted at them in a German accent. OK, it sounds corny – but it used to go down a treat at the end of the evening. Then one night the vice squad came in. They'd heard about my act and apparently they hadn't liked what they'd heard. They didn't mind you stripping as such but they had certain rules. You were supposed to keep your legs clamped together so you didn't show anything you shouldn't. Also you weren't supposed to whip the customers. I failed on both counts.

Well, the stupid guy from the vice squad sat right in the front. What an idiot! Of course, I didn't know he was vice squad and I went to town on him with the riding crop.

He came back to the club a week later with welts all over his face. He was black and blue. The boss showed him into my dressing-room without a word.

He was only quite a young bloke. He pointed to his face.

'Do you see what you did to me?' he asked. 'Do you know that I'm from the vice squad?'

I was indignant.

'Sweetheart, I never asked you to sit in the front,' I said. 'Anyway, you didn't identify yourself as vice squad.'

I thought he was just one of those mug punters who likes to sit in the front. They know what's going to happen – that's why they sit there.

'Well, I suppose that'll teach you something anyway,' I said with a smile. 'Never sit in the front when I'm on.'

I couldn't help treating it as a joke. He looked such a clot sitting there with little blue and pink stripes across his face. I wonder what he told his wife.

But I'd been warned, so I knew I had to be careful. I toned it down a bit after that till the heat died off.

By the end of my time in Liverpool I used to do shows for the police as well when they had special parties but I made sure I left the whip at home on these nights.

The Glad-Ray club was owned by two women called Gladys and Rachel, which explained the name. I think Gladys had started off working in a club herself but she had a good business head on her and now owned not only the Glad-Ray but a string of properties across Liverpool. She also acted as an agent for her girls, getting them work in other clubs if they wanted it. After I'd been a couple of months at the Glad-Ray Gladys asked if I'd like to rent a room at her house (she knew life was a bit crowded at Joyce's) and I jumped at the chance.

She was a great landlady. In the first place she taught me a lot about dancing. She used to give me tips on how to improve my act, but she also tried to improve my business sense and through her I learned how to make sure I got paid. She used to find me jobs in clubs all over Lancashire.

I hardly ever turned a job down. It wasn't really the money but the fact that I just enjoyed performing. I used to travel miles to get work. Once I danced on an American airbase near Warrington. At other times I'd do private shows for bands or other acts that were visiting Liverpool.

On one of these nights – it was a really famous band and they'd asked specially for me – the jukebox that we used in the private room broke down and I did the whole show without music because they said a good entertainer should be able to handle any crisis. So I just hummed the music away in my head and carried on. They gave me £50 and said, 'That's for a good show and being a good sport.'

Another night I remember especially came after a club manager phoned me at my landlady's one Sunday dinnertime. The club was at Garston, which was about ten miles away, and the manager said they needed a stripper in a hurry because the girl he'd booked hadn't turned up.

Gladys answered the phone and did all the negotiating. I heard her say, 'She's having her lunch.' Then after a long pause she said, 'Well, if she does decide to go you've got to give her two spots.' I used to get £5 a spot, so it made it more worthwhile to travel to a club if I appeared twice. Gladys was good like that. It seemed as though he agreed because she turned to me and said, 'Take it. Ten pounds is ten pounds.'

As usual I said yes and after tea Gladys drove me to the club. When I went in it was like walking into the Glad-Ray. All the fellows seemed to know me even though we were ten miles from my own club and there were shouts of 'Hiya, Gloria' as I came in through the door. 'All right. All right', I said. 'Cool it, boys. Let me get my knickers changed. Let me get myself prepared. I'll be out in a few minutes,' and I went into the dressing-room. I was just getting changed when who should turn up but the stripper the manager had booked in the first place. Five minutes later the manager walked into our room and said, 'Right, now that Susie's turned up, Gloria, you can have one spot.'

I shook my head. 'Oh no,' I said, 'you promised. I wouldn't have come all this bloody way to do one spot for five pounds. You said two spots.'

But he wasn't having it. 'No,' he said, 'I can't.' He waved towards the other girl. 'I've got to pay her for two spots already when she's only doing one because you're here.'

'OK, well forget it then,' I said, really annoyed. 'I'm going, but don't call *me* next time you're stuck. I don't want to work for you no more. Not ever again.'

He didn't seem bothered. 'All right,' he said with a shrug.

As I walked back out through the club there were all these surprised faces looking up at me.

'Where are you going, Gloria?' they called. 'We thought you were going to go on tonight.'

So I told them. I said, 'He tried to rip me off. He booked me for two spots because the girl hadn't turned up but now she's come and he only wants me to do one show, so I'm going home.'

One of the men said, 'No chance. We'll sort him out – get

yourself changed.' So back I went to the dressing-room and five minutes later the manager came in looking really cheesed off and said. 'OK, Gloria. Will you please do two spots for me tonight?'

'Certainly,' I said with a smile. 'Thank you so much.'

They were great, the Liverpool punters – very loyal. Once you got the respect of the Liverpool lads you were well away.

Although I was the no. 1 stripper at the Glad-Ray we'd often get girls from Manchester coming to give shows. They'd usually be very pretty girls with beautiful figures, while I had to be honest with myself: I was putting on quite a lot of weight in all directions. But in the Glad-Ray when these slim girls came on, the Liverpool punters would often be awful to them. They'd boo and say, 'Go on. Get off, you scrubber. Gloria! We want Gloria!' and they'd set up a chant. I'd try to hush them up because it was terrible for the other girls but inside I felt elated. 'Come on, Gloria,' they'd say, 'get up there and show her how it's done.' I bet they hated me, some of those strippers...

All the time I was working in Liverpool I kept in touch with Joyce, though once I'd moved into Gladys' house I didn't go back to Joyce's place much because her husband moaned about my being there. Although my mother was still living just down the road from Joyce I never asked about her, and because she knew how I felt Joyce never talked about her. I sometimes used to see Connie walking down the street, and I noticed that she had put a lot of weight on, but I didn't realize she was ill until Joyce met me in tears one night as I came out of the club. She said that Connie had died in hospital that night.

It seemed that the reason she'd suddenly got so fat was that her thyroid gland had gone wrong and she'd had to go into hospital for an operation, but maybe because of her heavy smoking over the years her heart had been weakened and she died soon after they finished the operation. I listened while Joyce told me what had happened and I felt cold and empty inside. I went home with Joyce that night and for the first time I talked about how I'd felt about Connie and how I'd never forgiven her for putting me in the children's home. That was when Joyce confessed that it wasn't Connie but she, Joyce, who had got in touch with them and asked them to take me.

'I did it for your own good, Gloria,' she kept saying. 'You were going to get killed, the way you were going on, running wild round the streets.'

As I listened to her I was stricken with a terrible guilt, realizing my mistake and trying to come to terms with the fact that I would never have the chance to say I was sorry to Connie now.

She was cremated two days later. I went to the crematorium with Thelma and Joyce and all of Connie's brothers and sisters and cried till I couldn't cry any more. It was the first time I'd cried for ages and I felt better for it. Joyce said I shouldn't feel so guilty: after all, Connie really hadn't cared for me very well and had only visited me twice while I was in the home, so it was understandable that I'd not liked her. I felt better when she said that – as though I'd been forgiven for what I'd done – and once I was back at the Glad-Ray I tried to put it all behind me.

It was shortly after this, while I was still feeling pretty depressed about Connie, that I met my first real boyfriend – by which I mean the first one that lasted more than a couple of months. His name was Ronnie. He was in his twenties and had been married, with two children, but the marriage had broken up. He was kind and said he understood when I talked about my mother dying and my mixed feelings about her. I was feeling very alone just then and he seemed to me to be just what I needed.

Soon after I met him he asked me to move in with him. Having learned my lesson by now, I went to the doctor and got put on the pill. Then, though I carried on working at the clubs, I moved into his house in Myrtle Street in Liverpool. Ronnie had a great sense of humour. He used to make me laugh a lot and he was generous to me, so I was really happy for the first few months we were together.

But then another side of Ronnie began to come out. He used to go out drinking at night with his mates, get tanked up and then come home really aggressive. If I said anything to upset him he'd start shouting at me and throwing me about. Sometimes I had to plaster make-up over my bruises before I could go on stage at the club. Twice I left him and went back to live with Gladys, but each time he came looking for me and begged me to go back, swearing he wouldn't hit me again. Each time I believed him and returned. I must have been mad but I stayed with him for nearly a year before I finally left him.

It's difficult to explain, but I can understand women who live like that for years and never leave. It takes the spirit out of you – the effort of getting away or doing anything about the mess you're in seems too much for you. It becomes easier to sit and take it than to do something about it.

But it was Gladys and the girls at the club who, in the end, made me see sense. I turned up for work once too often with bruises I couldn't hide and they finally persuaded me I'd be better off without Ronnie.

I knew that if I was going to make a break it would have to be a total one. It was no good carrying on at the Glad-Ray because Ronnie always came looking for me there after our rows. So I decided to leave Liverpool. I was getting restless again anyway, and one thing I couldn't stop thinking about was that I was 22 years old and I had never been abroad. This was the early 'seventies when package holidays had just taken off and everyone seemed to have been to Spain or Majorca for their summer hols.

I decided I would go to the south of France. It sounded classier than Majorca and I had made up my mind that I wanted to learn French. I thought I'd see where all the millionaires and movie stars go. So I got myself a passport, moved my things out of Ronnie's to Joyce's house, and took the train down to Dover. It was the first time I'd paid my fare to go down south in my life and it took a big chunk out of my savings, much of which had disappeared while I was living with Ronnie. I only had about £50 in my purse on the day I left Liverpool.

I took the ferry from Dover and then, once my feet touched French soil, I started hitching. I loved hitching, and you could do it then without feeling you were doing anything especially dangerous or risky. Or maybe it was just that I was younger and didn't worry so much about what might happen.

My first ride from Calais was with a truck driver. After that I got private cars. I got all the way down to the south of France in only four rides, and my last lift drove me all the way to Cannes. They were a Swiss couple. He was a lawyer and she was very bronzed and glamorous and they had a sports car. I climbed in the back. There wasn't much room but it was great. It was June and really hot and the wind blew through my hair. The further south we went the hotter it got and we kept stopping for cokes and lemonade. I had to pinch myself to make sure it was real.

As we got close to Cannes they asked if I had anywhere to stay. I said no and they said, 'OK, stay with us.' I couldn't believe my luck.

They made sure there was a spare bed in the hotel bedroom for me. Then they took me out for a meal and I pointed at the menu, with no idea what I was ordering. When it came it was a lovely steak. It wasn't till I finished that I asked what '*cheval*' meant and nearly brought it back up again when they told me.

'I can't eat horse.' I said. 'I used to ride them at the circus.'

But in spite of feeling guilty about the horse I slept really well that night. It had been a long time since I'd tasted good living. I wondered why I'd stuck out the last twelve months with Ronnie when life could be this good. The next day we went down to the hotel's private beach and I started wondering if I was too old to be adopted by these kind people I'd found.

But it wasn't to last. That evening the lawyer went into the bathroom to have a shower and while he was there his wife put her arm around me and tried to kiss me. I jumped as though I'd been stung. I couldn't understand it.

'Are you mad?' I said. 'I'm a woman. I've had a baby. I can't help you.'

I threw my things into my bag and shot out of the hotel like a rocket. Nothing like that had ever happened to me before and despite all my stripping and everything else I felt shocked.

So there I was with about 300 francs and no idea what I was going to do. My forward planning had never been too detailed. I lived on the basis that something would turn up and, sure enough, this time it did.

I went into a bar for a beer. I'd never been anywhere that was so hot before and I was incredibly thirsty all the time. I was standing at the bar knocking it back when suddenly a short, dark, foreign-looking man elbowed in beside me. He must have been about 40 and was starting to lose his hair; his waistline was going, too. He looked like a lot of the Glad-Ray customers in that respect.

He looked me up and down but that didn't bother me. I was used to it by now so I just stared back at him.

All of a sudden he spoke.

'Cinq mille?' he said, and he said it as though it were a question.

I said, 'What?' (My French had not progressed much in my two days in Cannes.)

He said again, *'Cinq mille?'*

I guessed I was being chatted up so I played along with him.

'Cinq mille. Is that a sort of drink or what?' I asked.

He looked blank.

'Do you speak English?' I asked him.

'Ah, Engleesh,' he said with a raise of his eyebrows.

Then he pushed his face towards mine and spoke again slowly. 'Five thousand. Five thousand francs. You understand?'

'For what?' I said. God, I was slow.

He smiled. 'For you and me. To go to hotel room.'

I said, 'Oh...'

I thought very quickly and the idea turned from being unpleasant to being very sensible indeed. After all, I'd often slept with men before when I'd have preferred not to.

To tell the truth, every time it had happened I'd have preferred not to. The only reason I'd ever done it was because the men wanted to – it was always to keep them happy. And all I'd got out of sleeping with men was pain: an infection that had nearly killed me; a baby that had nearly broken my heart; and a beating-up every other night. I felt suddenly angry with men – all the men who had ever used my body. In the past they'd satisfied themselves with me and I'd paid the price. What was so wrong with turning the tables on them?

I decided in that moment that it was a bloody good idea, especially as I was down to my last 300 francs.

'OK, come on then,' I said to the foreign guy.

We went to a hotel room. I was a bit embarrassed but I didn't let it show. I was also getting smart, no longer a dumb teenager, so I asked him for the money before he made a move. He handed it over without protesting and I zipped it away in my bag. Then I switched the light off and went over to the bed. He went to the other side. I took my clothes off in the dark and I could hear him doing the same on the other side of the bed. I took a deep breath, got on top of the covers and waited for it to be over. It was hardly any different from any other sex I had ever had. I didn't even pretend to be enjoying it. I just lay there and let him get on with it while I thought about what I was going to do with the money.

It was all over surprisingly quickly. He didn't kiss me, for which I was grateful, or speak. He just climbed on top of me, pushed himself quite gently into me and pumped away for a couple of minutes until he climaxed. Afterwards he lay there for a bit, lit a cigarette and passed me one. They were Gauloises and made me choke. Then he got up, took a shower and left with a wave and an *'au revoir'*. It was the most he'd said the whole time he was in the room.

I lay on the bed for a while thinking about what had happened and realized that for the first time ever I had felt some excitement while a man was making love to me. It wasn't sexual excitement, but a feeling of triumph that after all the pain they'd caused me I had discovered a way to get even with men. I didn't think of it as a career at that moment, but it had helped me out when I was short of money and I knew I could do it again if I needed to.

The next day I caught the train to Nice, rented a hotel room with the money I'd earned and put my mind to my ambition of learning French. Walking around Nice that day I came across an *au pair* agency and went in to see what it had to offer. It was run by a woman of about 60 who called herself La Professeuse. She said that what they did was to find suitable families for English girls to live with and then, two days a week, she ran French lessons at her office and all the *au pairs* met up there.

It sounded all right so I said I'd like to sign on with her. She wanted to know all about my past life and jobs before. I told her I'd been a stripper and she was highly amused. 'Only, oh, *s'il vous plaît*, don't tell *la famille* what you did before, OK?' she said, grinning wickedly at me.

'Pas de problème,' I said. I was picking up the lingo already.

She got me a job with a Swedish couple on the Avenue George Cinq. The woman turned out to be a real cow. She was a fanatic for cleaning and she had this parquet floor that she used to make me get down on my knees and polish every day. After an afternoon of that I used to fall into my bed at night.

I couldn't eat her food either. She bought beef a lot and it was always served half-cooked with blood running out all over the plate. Just looking at it made me sick. The beef I'd been brought up on, on the few occasions when he had beef, was always cooked for hours in the range at the home's kitchen and that was the way I liked it.

But not everything was bad. I started the language classes with the other *au pairs* and soon discovered that I had an ear for French, though my first lesson wasn't encouraging.

La Professeuse, who was very nice, introduced me to the other girls, but they were all on their seventh lesson. I sat down at my desk and she asked me a question in French.

'I don't understand,' I said. 'You'll have to speak in English.'

'Gloria,' she said in her strong French accent, 'I am asking you the question how many hours are there in one day?'

I couldn't resist it.

'Oh, well, that's easy,' I said. 'Twenty-four.'

All the girls started laughing.

'Oh, we 'ave a joker in the class, 'ave we?' said La Professeuse. But she was laughing too. She was all right. She was really a good friend by the time I left Nice.

I didn't stay with the Swedish couple long. I told La Professeuse I didn't like them and she found me a nice family who owned a supermarket in Monaco. They treated me really well. They had a lovely house without any parquet floors, so I was happy. I stayed with them for three months and by the end of that time I was speaking pretty good French. It seemed to come quite easily to me, and I wasn't embarrassed about trying it out the way some of the English *au pairs* were. I was coming top in the tests La Professeuse used to give us.

Then, for some reason, after about three months, although I was still having a good time I started getting homesick. I made up my mind to go back to England. The summer was nearly over anyway and the weather was getting colder.

The question was, where was home in England now? I decided to go to London. I didn't want to have to run into Ronnie again if I went back to the Glad-Ray, so I put together all my *au pair* money, caught a train back to London and found myself a room in a hotel in Sussex Gardens.

That left me just about broke and I had to think about a job. After France I had decided that as a way of earning money housework was not my scene. The obvious thing was stripping, but although I tried about a dozen clubs in the first week I was back none of them was looking for dancers. My fame obviously hadn't spread from Liverpool. No one seemed to have heard of the Glad-Ray when I mentioned it. I could have got a hostess job but the pay wasn't good.

I thought of the 5000 francs I'd earned so easily in the hotel room in Nice, and since money was now my priority – to buy my dreams of nice clothes and a nice place to live – the choice was a fairly easy one to make. I decided to start doing 'business'.

16

I hadn't much idea of how to set myself up to go 'on the game'. I was really naïve. I'd seen prostitutes hanging around in Soho, so I thought all I had to do was get myself a room and some sexy clothes and hang around with them. I was blissfully unaware that there were such things as territories, and pimps, or that prostitution was big business and was therefore run by quite smart businesmen who didn't appreciate girls on their own setting up in competition.

So, in happy ignorance, I bought some fancy outfits in Carnaby Street and started going down to Shepherd Market. And for a long time I got away with it. It was a case of fools rushing in, I suppose. I had no trouble finding clients. Men went to the Market looking for prostitutes and if you stood around for ten mminutes you could guarantee someone would come up to you and ask you, 'How much?' From talking to the other girls who worked there I discovered that the going rate for 'straight sex' was £20, so that was what I charged.

A lot of girls preferred to work in the afternoons because they felt it was safer. In my case I preferred it because I could enjoy going out on the town in the evening. After working out my expenses I decided that £60 a day was an acceptable income, so once I'd been with three clients I would shut up shop and get changed ready to go out and enjoy myself.

The hotel I found to work from in Sussex Gardens was owned by a Cypriot family. They knew what I was doing but as long as I paid my rent they didn't mind. I used to give them £2 out of every £20 I earned to keep them happy.

After a few weeks I started to get some regular clients – men who recognized me and came back for more. I don't know why, because when I started I was hardly the world's greatest lover. I didn't even pretend to enjoy sex. I just used to lie there as I had done the first time it happened in Cannes and think about something else. But after a while when I started doing business with the same men again I felt a bit guilty about taking their £20 off them and giving so little in return, so I began to act a bit – rolling my eyes and making moaning noises as they performed and telling them how good they were. I don't suppose it really fooled any of them but they seemed to like it.

Among my regular customers I soon picked up some real weirdos. Before I worked in Shepherd Market I had no idea there were such peculiar blokes walking about the streets. And the funny thing was, you'd never have known if you'd met them, say, at a party. They nearly all looked quite normal. It was only when they asked for special services that their strange kinks were revealed.

One guy used to like me to wrestle naked with him. God, the punishment I took! But he always liked me to win in the end. That was part of the agreement. I used to pin him against the wall and hold his arms behind his back while he begged for mercy. It was his fantasy that we were in a wrestling ring together in front of the TV cameras. In fact he wouldn't have known the difference between a Boston Crab and a boiled lobster, but I went along with it. He paid me £30 a time so I could afford to be generous to him.

Another regular was a schoolteacher – at least, he *said* he was a schoolteacher, unless that was all a part of his fantasy too. He used to spank me with his hand across my bare backside and boy! he didn't mess about. He always wanted to give me twenty slaps but I only used to last till ten most times. And all the time he was slapping me he'd be saying, 'You naughty girl! You naughty girl!' Often he would hurt me so much that I could hardly sit down afterwards, but in a funny sort of way I liked it – it didn't excite me, but I felt better after he'd given me a good belting. It was as if I had been punished for what I was doing.

If I was honest with myself I knew I was unhappy about being a prostitute. I was confused. Part of me wanted to do it and part of me felt guilty and ashamed about it. But I didn't feel guilty enough to stop. I'd think about the clothes I was able to buy now – the nice shoes, the expensive silk underwear and the fur coat I was saving for – and I was able to put my conscience back to sleep without too much trouble.

And in any case it wasn't all unpleasant. Some of it was really . funny. One of my clients liked me to throw cream cakes at him. He was a little man, going bald, very well-dressed and smart and ever so polite. He used to arrive carrying a cardboard cake-box tied up with that plastic string they use in cake shops and when he'd got undressed I'd have to pelt him with cream puffs and chocolate eclairs. It made a mess and took a while to clear up the room, but that was all I objected to; apart from that I didn't really mind doing it. Specials were always £30 and for that sort of money I'd have thrown Black Forest gâteaux at him if he'd wanted me to.

There was another client who wanted me to smack him. But he didn't want sex afterwards – the pain was all he was interested in. He used to take off his trousers and bend over a chair in the corner of the room and I would hit him with the back of a wooden clothes-brush until I was out of breath. To keep myself going I used to imagine he was all the men I hated most in my life rolled into one: Uncle John, and the man who gave me gonorrhoea, and Ronnie, who used to hit me when he got drunk. I'd smack away at his bony little white backside until my arm hurt – and he never even whimpered. I couldn't understand it, but I didn't think about it too deeply. I felt it was none of my business. I couldn't understand what pleasure people got from normal sex, let along kinky sex, so I just went along with whatever they wanted and didn't ask questions.

I used to feel quite sorry for some of them. Once I got to know them I realized that most of them weren't a bit like the men who'd treated me badly. They were often timid, shy men and usually they were very nice and polite to me before and after doing business.

It was probably because of this that I never felt frightened.

However strange they were in their fetishes and fantasies it never occurred to me that my clients might harm me. Most of them, apart from the schoolteacher, only seemed to be interested in violence if it was being done to *them* and they wouldn't have hurt a fly. I knew that from time to time girls did get beaten up or even killed, but it was very rare and I certainly never worried about it.

There were other dangers in being a prostitute though, apart from violence. You could catch VD or get pregnant if you weren't careful, as lots of girls used to find out. But although I had made nearly all the mistakes in the book in my life so far, I had usually made them only once and I was taking no chance of getting caught like that again. I used to keep packets of Durex in the cupboard beside my bed and I'd make each customer put one on, or else I'd put one on for him if he preferred.

I carried on like this for about a year, living quite well by catering for just three clients a day; but sometimes, if I wanted to buy something expensive, I'd take a few more. The only time I really went over the top was the first Christmas I was back in London. Joyce had invited me to go to Liverpool for Christmas week and stay with her. I wanted to buy something really nice for my sister's kids so I worked non-stop during the two days before I left London. I must have taken nearly £400. Then I went out and bought teddy bears and dolls and boxes of Lego and piled them all into a big hold-all to take with me. Joyce had seven children by now so I ended up with quite a collection of stuff.

Joyce couldn't believe it when she saw it all and wanted to know what I was doing to have been able to afford it. I didn't tell her at first. I said I was just hostessing, but a couple of days before Christmas, after a few drinks, I confessed I was street-walking and that I had slept with about twenty men in order to get the money together to pay for the presents.

She looked puzzled rather than shocked and kept saying, 'But *why* did you want to do that? You didn't have to buy all these things for the kids. Why do you have to try and *buy* our love all the time, Gloria?'

'Because I don't know how else to get it,' I burst out, upset by the way I felt she was rejecting me. 'I don't know any other way.' And to my shame I started to cry.

It was the drink talking. Normally I would never have let Joyce see how much I felt I needed my family's approval. I had to admit that what she said was partly true. Ever since I was a child, whenever I wanted affection, I had tried to win it by giving presents. It had started with the handkerchiefs for Auntie Sandra and carried on ever since.

But I wasn't just trying to buy Joyce's family's love. There was something else involved in my present-giving; it was also a way of showing my own affection, and Joyce didn't seem to understand that. Of course I wanted her kids to like me, but as well as that I wanted them to know that *I* liked *them*. It was important for kids to feel loved. I knew that fact perhaps better than Joyce, but she couldn't believe that that was why I'd done it. I think she thought I was just trying to show her up by bringing bigger and better presents than she and her husband had got for the kids themselves. They were very hard up and I can see now that I must have made them feel rotten when they saw their own small presents next to the ones I'd bought. Perhaps it hadn't been very tactful of me, but at the time it hadn't crossed my mind what Joyce would think. I'd just been thinking of the kids.

The result was that Christmas was not the happy time I'd looked forward to. There was an atmosphere hanging over us. Joyce's husband Lawrence had never liked me and on Christmas Eve Joyce, who was still upset at me, told him how I had made the money to get the toys. He blew his top and told me to get out of his house and not come back, ever. Joyce got upset then and tried to calm him down, saying she hadn't meant it to end up like this, but Lawrence turned on her and hit her. I ran upstairs, grabbed my bags and ran out of the house.

Outside it was cold and it had actually started snowing – for the first time in years on Christmas Eve in Liverpool. I started walking towards town, not knowing what I was going to do or where I was going to sleep. I was overwhelmed by a feeling of wanting to die. Everything I did seemed to backfire on me and be misunderstood. However much I tried, I was never able to get it right. At that moment, in the middle of Walton, I hated myself. I stood sobbing on the pavement with people rushing past me and felt in my handbag for the packet of razor blades I'd bought that morning to shave my legs. I unwrapped the paper. Then, with my brain numb and my heart pounding, I started to slash again and again at my wrists. You're not supposed to feel a really sharp blade but I felt it all right and was glad. I wanted it to hurt. I felt I deserved it.

For a while, no one noticed what I was doing, even though there seemed to be blood everywhere, then I staggered off the pavement into the path of a car. Hands rushed to grab me as I fell over and everything went black until I woke up in hospital a couple of hours later.

I was in a bed with curtains around me. My wrists were bandaged and my head hurt, but apart from that I seemed to be all right. I thought about what had happened and felt embarrassed when I remembered what I'd done. It was as though another person had been in my body. I couldn't imagine now, in the cold, sober atmosphere of the hospital ward, why I should have behaved the way I did. It seemed stupid and childish and I didn't want to think about it.

Joyce came to the hospital that night. Some people who had recognized me had gone round to her house and told her what had happened. She was in tears and kept apologizing, but I said it wasn't her fault, it was mine, and after a bit she went away again because it was Christmas Eve and she had to pack the kids' Christmas stockings. I suddenly remembered that it had been on Christmas Eve when I was sixteen that I had tried to end it all by drinking a cupful of Vim, and I wondered why Christmas often had this depressing effect on me.

Nurses came and went and took my blood pressure and temperature but no one said anything to me except that 'the doctor' would be seeing me later. He came the next morning and asked me lots of questions about why I'd done it, which I wasn't able to answer.

Over the next two days as they carried on with their questioning, memories of Mostyn Nerve Hospital kept floating into my head. The anger and despair I'd felt on Christmas Eve had changed. I didn't feel ill or particularly depressed now, just a bit tired and fed-up, and I didn't want to spend the next three months drawing pictures for psychiatrists. The obvious thing seemed to be to go. So the day after Boxing Day I got dressed, walked shakily to the desk and discharged myself.

They tried to stop me, but people in authority didn't frighten me any more. I knew they had no right to keep me there. I collected my case, caught a taxi to the train and set off for London.

Back in my room in Sussex Gardens I didn't work for two weeks while my wrists healed. When the bandages came off, though, the scars were still obvious, so as soon as I started taking clients again I had to make up stories to explain them when people noticed them and got curious. Usually I said I'd had an operation to remove cysts and that seemed to satisfy most of them.

Thelma came down to London to visit me when she found out what had happened and Joyce telephoned me regularly to see how I was, which meant a lot to me. It wasn't really Joyce who had upset me so much as her husband, anyway, so we decided I'd keep away from him from now on and only visit Joyce if he wasn't going to be at home. Gradually over the next few months I put the memory of that awful evening behind me and concentrated on building up my circle of friends in London. If I had more friends of my own, I told myself, then I wouldn't be so upset another time if my family turned against me.

Whenever I wasn't working I liked to hang around Carnaby Street. I used to drink in one of the bars there, and there was a shop run by a queer called Dudley where I used to buy a lot of my clothes. He was really kind. He always used to make time to have a gossip with me when I came in. He'd talk about who'd been into the shop and what shows he'd seen recently. He seemed to have a lot of influential friends, to whom he'd introduce me when they were in the shop.

One of them was an actor who was playing at the Savoy. I met him and his wife at the shop and had dinner with them at their house. I even slept there a few times. They knew what I was doing for a living because Dudley had told them but they were still friendly to me. They tried to get me to give up prostitution, saying I was too nice to do that kind of work, but I just laughed, embarrassed, and said I would give it up as soon as I could afford to.

I didn't like talking about it much, as I had done when I was stripping. I wouldn't have minded them knowing about that, but prostitution was different. I did it, but I wasn't proud of it. I didn't want the world to know.

There was another couple I met at the shop. The woman was quite a well-known opera singer from America. She was called Wendy and her nickname for the man was Peter Pan, so they used to call me Tinkerbell. He was an artist. They took me to the theatre and the cinema with them – I remember going with them to see *Alice Doesn't Live Here Any More* with Ellen Burstyn, which I thought was brilliant.

Shortly after that I met some even more famous people. After Christmas I had started working in the evenings sometimes instead of the afternoons and if I was going to Shepherd Market at night I used to have a drink first in a bar in Carnaby Street. I wouldn't be looking for business, just having a few drinks to give me the nerve to go out and get started. I was never able to find work without having a couple of drinks first during the whole time I did business.

I was sitting there as usual one night, knocking back my gin and tonic, when my eyes nearly popped out of my head. The pop group Hot Chocolate had just walked into the bar. I couldn't believe it, because I loved their music. The first thing I'd bought with my earnings when I set up as a prostitute was a stereo record-player and some LPs. Hot Chocolate were my favourite group. I called, 'Hello' up the bar to them and told them I'd got their records, and in no time at all I was talking to them. Larry, who played the organ, turned out to have the star sign Aries just like me. I was very keen on astrology at the time and so was he, so we got on like a house on fire.

Then, after a bit, they started looking at their watches. 'Come on,' they said to me. 'Let's go up and have a drink at Shepherd Market.'

'OK,' I agreed. 'It's on my way to work.'

'What?' asked Larry, curiously.

For once I decided to be brazen about it.

'Yes, I walk the pavements. I'm a lady of the streets,' I said, waiting a bit nervously for their reaction.

They weren't bothered. 'Oh well, it's an honest profession,' one of them said. 'But leave it for tonight. Come with us to Gulliver's.'

Gulliver's was a club near the Hilton. All the pop stars used to go there. I didn't need asking twice. I thought of one of the girls I was friendly with. I knew she'd love it.

'Can I bring a friend?' I asked.

'OK,' they said. 'See you there at nine.'

I couldn't believe it. I went back to the flat, changed and rang my friend to arrange to meet her. At first she thought I was kidding when I said we'd been invited out by Hot Chocolate, but she finally agreed to meet me at 8.30 at Shepherd Market.

I was waiting on the corner for her, nearly dancing in the street with excitement, when a police car came down the road. They were always on patrol, looking for kerb-crawlers and girls soliciting. I knew they recognized me now and they had no doubts about what I was up to when I was in the Market, but so far I'd managed to steer clear of trouble with them. Now, as I watched, a copper leaned out of the car window and pointed down the road with his thumb.

'Come on, you. Move,' he said.

'Don't worry,' I answered, sticking my nose in the air. 'I'm not working tonight. It's my night off. I'm waiting for a friend.' So on they went.

And then, two minutes later, another police car came by. This time it stopped and a copper got out and came towards me.

'Right, you – you're nicked,' he said.

'No, please, no,' I wailed. I couldn't believe this was happening to me. It was so unfair. I almost went down on my knees to them, I was so desperate.

'I'm not working tonight. Don't nick me tonight. I'm waiting for my friend. We're meeting Hot Chocolate. Please...'

They wouldn't listen. They nicked me and my evening was ruined. I was really upset. What bothered me most was that Hot Chocolate would think I'd stood them up. It really mattered to me, that, because they had seemed to like me. I didn't want them to think I'd do a thing like that to them.

I was taken to West End Central Police Station and kept in overnight. The next day the magistrates fined me £10 for soliciting. I never did pay the fine because I wasn't soliciting – not when they caught me. I'd been wearing my best nightclub dress, which was very classy; I still had it on next morning when they let me out, so I don't think I'd even looked like a prostitute that night, but the police knew me – that was my downfall.

It's strange, but it still upsets me to think about that evening. I used to love meeting famous people. When I was with them it was as if a little bit of their glamour and life-style rubbed off on me. I used to think about the people in the children's home and it was like that Shirley MacLaine song in the film *Sweet Charity,* the one that goes, 'They'd never believe it, if my friends could see me now', which she sings after she gets picked up by the rich and famous star. I loved that song – though it wasn't my friends I was thinking about, it was Uncle John. The words summed up the way I'd felt when I was chatting to Larry from Hot Chocolate.

It was about three months after the Hot Chocolate fiasco that I was beaten up by the pimp Spiros and the police painted themselves even blacker in my eyes by saying that they couldn't help me. That night was a sort of turning point in a way and made me decide to give up prostitution for the time being, though it was more through fear than from remorse at having been a 'bad girl'.

After I left the police station that night I sneaked back to my hotel room. I knew I was taking a chance but I guessed that the last place Spiros would think I'd hide from him would be in his own hotel. I was right. He was still out when I got there, either looking for me or getting drunk with his friends. I picked up as many of my things as I could cram into my cases. I had to leave my stereo and records behind but I pulled the arm off the stereo and smashed as many of the records as I could so Spiros couldn't use them. Then I ran out of the front door like a bat out of hell.

I took a taxi to the other side of London and checked into a hotel and there I stayed for the next week. It was awful. I couldn't work, even if I'd wanted to, because of my ribs hurting, and I was afraid to leave the hotel even to see a doctor. It was years later, after I'd had an X-ray for something else, that I was told that my ribs had actually been broken.

I was starting to imagine that Spiros had spies out all over London looking for me. I was paranoid whenever anyone looked at me in the hotel wondering if it was one of his friends. I knew it was ridiculous and I knew I would drive myself crazy if I went on like this. The solution was to go away somewhere, but where? A few days later, I was looking through a travel brochure in the hotel lounge when a picture of a temple set against a blue sky sprang out of the page at me. This gave me the answer, instantly. After all, it was time I saw the sun again. I decided I would go to Greece.

17

The ticket to Greece cost me £25, which was for an overland trip by bus. I thought of flying, but after paying a week's hotel bills with no money coming in I was getting very close to being hard-up. Although I'd been earning a lot of money over the past year I'd been spending it pretty freely, too, and what with stereos and fox-furs I'd never had much left over to put in the bank for a rainy day. I thought I'd better count the pennies till I knew what I was going to do next. For the same reason I didn't get a return ticket. I would have to earn some money in Greece to take care of that.

The bus left London on Wednesday morning. I'd got friendly with a boy staying at my new hotel and had told him about Spiros, and this boy took me to the bus station in his car. I found a seat away from the window and as the bus pulled away from the terminal I started to relax for the first time since I'd been beaten up. Even so, it wasn't until we had crossed the Channel on the ferry and were driving off at Calais that I really felt safe. When that happened I fell asleep for the first time in a week and missed most of the drive through France.

The trip took three days. I wouldn't recommend it as the ideal way of reaching Greece, but it was cheap.

I met an English girl on the bus who was going out to be nanny to a Greek family. I think she'd answered an advertisement. She asked why I didn't try it, and I said I thought I might. It would at least give me a roof over my head while I decided what I was going to do for the rest of the time. She gave me the address of the agency in Athens who had fixed up her job, and soon after arriving there I went looking for it. It seemed the agency couldn't get enough English girls to work as nannies and the staff had no trouble in finding me a family, though the job was only for three months. I was employed to look after two little girls aged four and fifteen months in an apartment in Athens. They were lovely kids, happy and well-behaved, so I enjoyed it. The mother was a bit domineering and her own mother lived with them as well and was even worse. She was always interfering, so there were a lot of noisy rows all the time. I just used to keep out of the way and play outside with the children, so it didn't bother me that much.

I didn't get a lot of time off but whenever I had a free hour I used to go sightseeing in Athens. I'd enjoyed the south of France, but I soon discovered that Greece was different again and after my first week I had fallen in love with it. It wasn't just the fantastic ancient monuments. It was the people, who always seemed so friendly and talkative and welcoming. I felt at home among them right from the start, so much so that I wondered if I might have Greek blood in my veins.

I had been nannying for two months when I met some Lebanese girls at a café who told me they were cabaret dancers at a club in Athens. I got talking to one of them in particular who was called Nadia. She was really beautiful and a very good dancer, as I found out later.

'What are you doing in Greece?' she asked me.

'Nothing much – just being a nanny. But that finishes in a few weeks,' I answered.

'Well, why don't you work in a club like us?' she said.

Ding! A bell rang in my head. That was the answer. I hadn't even known that they had clubs in Greece. I thought they were very strict and didn't allow things like that.

So Nadia took me to meet her agent – an Arab called Anwar. I didn't like him. He looked shifty and practically the first thing he said to me was that he took ten per cent commission, but he was able to find me a job working with Nadia so I decided to put up with him for the time being.

He found us work in a club called the Rainbow Bar in Piraeus, the port just south of Athens. During the time I worked there I made another friend, a girl called Maria who was from the Seychelles – there were girls from all over the world in the club business. It was like a big women's association – not the Girl Guides or the Women's Institutes exactly but still a friendly sort of group. I used to feel I had something in common with a hostess or dancer no matter where they came from. It was as though you spoke the same secret language.

In fact the language that most of them *did* speak was Greek, since you couldn't get very far in chatting up the local customers without it. I was a hostess at the Rainbow Club, which was similar to being a hostess in London in that you had to get them to buy drinks but quite different from London in that the men weren't always trying to chat you up or touch you. They just seemed to like to have a pretty girl around while they were drinking with their friends, and usually you'd sit and talk with a group of them rather than pick on one man as you did in the London clubs. I learned enough Greek to get by very quickly. Once I'd heard a new word I never forgot it and I used to practise new sentences every day and ask the customers if I'd got it right, and they'd laugh and help me with my pronunciation. After two months I was beginning to think that I had missed my vocation. Maybe I could have become a United Nations translator. But I wasn't complaining. Being a hostess at the Rainbow Club suited me fine. I was enjoying myself.

But my time was running out. I only had a visa for six months and I needed to apply for an extension for another six months. This wasn't as easy as it sounded as for some reason you had to apply for the extension from outside Greece. The other girls told me that the agent would usually arrange that you could go to Yugoslavia and put in your application from the consulate there. I kept asking Anwar to do this and he kept promising to arrange it, but when my visa had only two weeks to run and Anwar was still taking ten per cent of my wages but doing nothing about the extension I decided to change my agent.

I found a new one quite easily and immediately wondered why I hadn't done it sooner. My new agent, Diamandis, was a Greek of about 60 and he was lovely – he really took care of his girls. He was able to fix up for me to go to Yugoslavia straight away and a week later I took the train from Athens.

I had thought it would be like going from Liverpool to London, but I hadn't looked at the map. It was 24 hours before I stepped off the train in Skopje. I didn't mind, though. It was like a big adventure, a geography lesson come to life. I drank it all in – the strange smells, the unfamiliar scenery, the peasants bringing chickens and ducks and even goats on to the train. I sat and watched open-mouthed and thought of how I'd lived all those years in that cold, grey house in England, never knowing that life could be like this, full of fascinating sights and sounds and friendly, smiling people, and with warm air and blue skies all the time instead of sleet and fog and rain. I decided I would like to live in Greece forever.

When at last we got to Skopje it was like a shanty town and I wasn't tempted to stay long. I just filled in my visa form as my agent had said, handed it in at the Embassy and caught the train straight back to Athens again. Once I had returned safely Diamandis said I was to move from the Rainbow Club and he found me a job in another place in Piraeus called John Bull's. This was a much bigger club than my last one but it was still fun to work in. It wasn't an English club, despite its name, and I think the owner was Greek, though we didn't see much of him.

There was a mama at the club – a small, fat Greek woman who used to look after all the girls. She was great. She used to go round selling nuts and checking that you weren't having any trouble, and she was wonderful at sorting out any men who were causing problems – not that that often happened. The Greek men could make a lot of noise but there wasn't often any violence. It was a nice atmosphere at the John Bull, just as it had been at the Rainbow Club. Some of the girls used to do a bit of business but you didn't have to, so I didn't. I'd had enough of that for the time being. I concentrated instead on having a good time – which wasn't hard there.

We didn't start work until late afternoon, so during the day most of the girls would go down to the beach and get a sun-tan. My skin gradually turned a deep brown. I couldn't get over it. I'd never been tanned before. Even when I worked in Nice I was doing housework during the day so I didn't get much time on the beach. I made up for it now, and discovered that a tan suited me. Normally I was very pale and with my black hair I often looked ill even when I wasn't. Now I'd found the sun I always looked the picture of health.

Even when I had to drag myself off the beach and start work it wasn't too much of an effort. Most of the time when you worked in the club it was just like being taken out for a drink. The Greek men didn't try to grope you when they'd had a bit to drink – unlike English men. The most they might do was put their arms round you, but they did that with each other too so that was OK. It was tame.

I was working on commission. My basic wage was 2,500 drachmas a day, but for each bottle of champagne drunk by the men I was with I'd get another 1,000 drachmas. For whisky I'd be paid 100 drachmas a glass or 1,000 drachmas a bottle. On a good night I could earn 9,000 drachmas. It was a lot of money and living in Greece was cheap. My hotel only cost 300 drachmas a day and a good meal was about 100 drachmas, so I was able to save quite a lot.

In order to collect your commission you had to wait till the men had drunk the whole bottle – of whisky or whatever – then you'd take it to the bar when you went to get another bottle and the barman would mark it down to you for commission. Obviously, a quick way to get the bottle empty was to drink a lot of it yourself, but you couldn't keep that up forever, so when I thought the men weren't looking I used to empty my glass under the table and push it over to be filled again.

One night when I was with four men and doing this, one of them turned to me and said in Greek, 'Gloria, do you *like* sitting with us at this table?'

'Yes, of course,' I said, surprised he should ask when I thought I was being the life and soul of the party.

He smiled.

'We like having you here too,' he said. Then he leaned towards me and whispered in my ear, 'But don't throw the whisky away, OK? We'll drink that. We can drink fast enough if that's what you want. Did you think we're so drunk we don't see?'

I felt like a little girl caught being naughty by a teacher. I didn't know what to say. I thought he was angry and was going to cause trouble.

But instead he laughed. 'We don't want you to have a headache, Gloria. You shouldn't have to drink whisky if you don't like it.' Then he whispered again: 'Look, if you want, you drink Coca-Cola and we'll drink faster – then we'll all be happy, OK?'

After that, I ordered Coca-Cola whenever I was with them, which was good. No one else bought their girls Coca-Cola. When the other girls had had enough whisky they had to drink water.

There was another group of men I used to drink with regularly. There were five of them and they were great royalists. They all loved King Constantine and they used to talk to me about the queen of England and how wonderful they thought our royal family was, and we'd always end the evening by toasting the queen of England and the king of Greece in whisky.

There were some Thai girls working as hostesses at the John Bull and they were very sneaky. They'd see you sitting down at a table with some men, watch you until you'd finished nearly all the whisky in the bottle, then come up to your table smiling sweetly.

'Ah-hah, hello. I sit down and join you?' they'd say and they'd sit down before anyone could answer. 'I help you finish the bottle?' they'd ask.

'Oh yes, sure,' I'd think. 'Then you can take half my commission. I've polished it all off and you collect – very smart.'

But of course I could only think it. I couldn't say anything out loud. You were supposed to let the men kid themselves that you were drinking with them because you liked their company. But these four guys were great. They understood.

'Oh, fine,' they'd say. 'Sit down and join us – as long as you don't mind if Gloria takes the commission.'

The Thai girls didn't like that. 'Oh, no, no!' they'd say, backing off. 'Maybe better she stay here alone with you,' and they'd slink off, full of Eastern promise, to try to free-load on someone else.

I remember one time I was sitting at the table and these fans of

King Constantine were watching the cabaret. I had had enough whisky for the night, so I tried the old whisky-throwing trick with them but it went badly wrong, probably because I'd already drunk too much of the whisky before I started throwing it away and my hand was a bit unsteady. I had filled my glass and emptied it under the table about five times when suddenly the guy sitting next to me tapped me on the shoulder.

'Gloria,' he said. 'It's very good you don't drink too much or you'll be ill, but if you're going to throw it then throw it on the floor – not on my pants, please.' When he stood up I could see that his trousers were soaked in whisky. He must have smelled like a distillery when he got home. Luckily for me they all thought it was funny, but for the next round I was back on water.

I didn't do any dancing while I was at the John Bull. They had quite a lot of cabaret acts but mostly with groups of girls, not strippers, and I didn't want to be one of a chorus line. For the time being I was content just to be a hostess and put money in the bank. There was another thing stopping me dancing, too – the fact that I now had a boyfriend. His name was Thomas. I'd met him in the hotel where I lived with the other cabaret girls. The Hotel Egina was a great place – more like a club than most people's idea of a hotel – and we could cook our own food there, which made the cost of living even cheaper.

I'd met Thomas in the hotel's big pool room one night. He came in with a friend and after they'd played pool for a bit they started talking to Maria and me. I think I fell in love for the first time in my life that night. Thomas was 6 feet 2 inches tall with black curly hair and enormous brown eyes. He was so good-looking I couldn't keep my eyes off him while he was playing pool, and I couldn't remember that ever happening with a man before. I discovered he was a Libra, which meant he was artistic and a practical joker, which I liked.

He told me he was attending Naval College, with the intention of becoming a First Officer in the Merchant Navy, and his father was paying for his studies. He said he had to go to night school that night but he'd like it if I could go out with him the following night. I told him what work I did. There was no point in trying to hide it. It was bound to come out sooner or later, so I thought I might as well come clean straight away. Fortunately he said he didn't mind.

I took the evening off the following night for our date and the whole time we were together I felt I was walking on air. I think Thomas felt the same way about me. He told me later that the first night when he'd said he had to go to night school he was really meeting a girl, but he'd told her on that occasion that he wasn't going to see her any more because he'd met someone else who was special.

After our date Thomas came back with me to the Hotel Egina and stayed the night, and after that he spent most of his nights with me and brought his things to my hotel room. We stayed together for six months: he'd go off to college during the day and then join me at the hotel after I finished work at the club.

Thomas explained that he didn't mind my being a hostess because I wore a dress for that and he knew all I did was talk to the men, but he wasn't keen on the idea of my dancing or taking my clothes off at the club so I went along with what he wanted. I liked him more than I'd ever liked anyone before and I didn't want to do anything to upset him.

I got on well with Thomas's family – his sister Fotonulia (Fo-Fo for short) and brother Dmitri. Dmitri lived at home with Thomas's parents, and at first everything went well when I met his mother and father too. But there was trouble when Thomas's father found out I was working as a hostess. He was a politician and very conservative and he told Thomas that hostesses and cabaret girls were the biggest whores you could find, so after that we had to keep secret that we were still seeing each other and Thomas pretended he was staying at the college or going to his sister's house whenever he was staying with me. The funny thing was that his mother didn't mind about me – but in Greek households the man is the boss, so there wasn't much she could do to help us.

Not surprisingly, considering the amount of time we were

spending together, Thomas neglected his studies. One day the head of the college told him that he had to stay in residence over the weekend to catch up on his work for the final exams. Thomas got annoyed at being treated like a child and slipped out on the Saturday night so that he could be with me, but when he tried to sneak back in he was caught. The head suspended him for two months, which meant he would have to sit the exams late and on his own.

His father was livid and I suppose you couldn't blame him. I was upset, too. I didn't want to think that I'd been the cause of Thomas losing his chance of a career. I really wanted him to become a First Officer. I loved him in his naval cadet's uniform. He looked so smart. I knew he would look twice as good in an officer's uniform.

We decided that he would be sensible and really work hard in September for the three weeks before his exams, but in the meantime we spent the summer enjoying ourselves. He was very popular, with a big crowd of friends, and every day a large group of us would go to the cinema or to the beach and afterwards to one of the cafés for pizza. It was good, my first real love affair.

In September he took his exams and passed them. We had a great celebration, but although I joined in all the celebrations I was sad at the same time. I'd always known that when he joined the Merchant Navy I would lose Thomas, and soon after he got his exam results he heard that he had a position on a ship and would have to join it in New York.

But our time together had to end anyway. The same week that Thomas was due to leave, my visa ran out, and there was no way of getting a second extension. I begged my agent to find a way, but he said there was nothing for it but for me to leave Greece. He said if I'd never had a visa then maybe he could have helped me, but because I'd done it all legally the first time the police would know I was there and would track me down if I started working without the proper papers.

Thomas and I went out for a farewell dinner the night before he left. I felt really depressed. It wasn't just because of Thomas, but because of Greece itself. I'd grown to love it and its people. It felt more of a home to me after that short time than anywhere else I'd ever lived in my life.

Even so, I knew enough about the country to know that I didn't want to spend six months in a Greek prison, so three days after Thomas flew off to New York I packed up my things once more and left by train for Liverpool.

18

Back in Liverpool my life came down to earth with a bump. The days of sun and sand were over. I moved in with Joyce, who by now had left Lawrence and had a house in another district of Liverpool, Huyton. I had quite a lot of money saved from working in Greece, though not exactly enough to retire on, and I started to look for work. The trouble was that after Greece all the Liverpool clubs struck me as boring and depressing and I didn't fancy working in them again. The atmosphere wasn't the same.

Joyce had taken all her seven children with her when she left Lawrence, so the house was crowded enough before I moved in. To get out from under Joyce's feet I used to go out most evenings to the pub down the road and I got to know a girl called Lizzie there. After I had been chatting to her for a few nights I noticed that she always left the pub about the same time, 9.30, saying she was going to see her boyfriend. I asked her one night if he worked shifts – at which she laughed. She said she had a boyfriend on a ship in the docks and spent each night on board with him. She suggested I went along with her the next night to see if I could find a sailor boyfriend too.

'They look after you all right, the sailors,' she said, winking at me, 'and they get well paid, too.'

'Why not?' I thought.

And so the following night I went with Lizzie to the docks and was introduced to the old Liverpool custom of ship-visiting. Really, of course, it was prostitution again, but a different sort of prostitution from what I'd been doing in London. It was like having a boyfriend for maybe two weeks at a time, which was the period each ship stayed in the port. You didn't sleep around on the ship usually. It was one man at a time and instead of paying you before you went to bed with them they'd share their pay with you when they got it, so you could pretend to yourself that it wasn't really sex they were paying you for at all. Because of that it felt a bit more respectable than walking the streets.

Sometimes, I discovered, you had to work on credit if they hadn't been paid when you met them, but usually they were very straight, the sailors. You always got paid in the end. It was true you couldn't earn as much as you could in London, but then there was no hotel bill to pay so you didn't do so badly.

Over the years the girls in the area had developed quite a system for ship-visiting, which I soon cottoned on to. It wasn't just a matter of walking on board, because the port authorities knew what was going on and they didn't encourage it, to put it mildly.

The first problem was getting on to the dock area. There was a security fence all round it and the dock police would check all the cars going in to see what their business was. It was quite clever, the way we used to sneak through. We had a special arrangement with the taxis: the drivers would stop just before they got to the dock entrance and the girls – there would usually be two of us travelling together – would climb into the boot. Most of the drivers even used to carry a pillow and a bit of carpet in the boot to make it more comfortable for the girls. Then they'd drive on through the dockyard gates and tell the men on duty they were coming to pick someone up off a ship.

Sometimes, of course, the dock police would look in the car boot and then the game would be up, but that's all it was to them – a game. They didn't arrest us. They'd just send us on our way and ten minutes later we'd find another taxi and try again. We used to give the taxi-drivers whisky and cigarettes that we'd got off the boat and pay them good tips so that it would be worth their while to do it.

Once we'd got through the gates, if we were looking for a new 'boyfriend' we'd tell the taxi-driver to drive around and we'd look at all the flags. You could tell from the flags which ships they were and Lizzie soon put me right on which were the best ships. The favourite, while I was working there, was the *Inca Capac*, which was from Peru. The South Americans were supposed to be the most generous and treat you the best. After them, the Greeks and the Chinese were also pretty good.

When you'd decided on a ship you'd get out of the taxi and sneak up the gangway when you thought no one was looking. If you could get on board without being spotted you were home and dry. Once you were on a ship no one would throw you off. The next thing you'd do would be to ask someone on the ship to show you where the men ate. Usually you'd have gone on board with another girl and the two of you would go along to the canteen, get a cup of tea or a beer and sit down and look for someone to start chatting to. It would never take long for someone to come over. The men all knew why you were there. Then after you'd had a few drinks with a bloke and chatted to him for a bit you'd go back with him to his cabin and you'd be fixed up for the next fortnight. Easy!

Some of the girls didn't even bother leaving the boat for the two weeks it was in port because it was too much hassle getting back on to the docks every day. So they'd just take a suitcase with them the first day they went on board and that was it. I did it myself a few times. It depended which ship you were on, whether you wanted to take a break. If it was a Greek ship, I almost never went back to Joyce's house until it left port again. I used to love them. They were like floating hotels, the Greek ships. You'd wake up in the morning and whoever you were with would bring your breakfast and a cup of tea while you lay in your bunk. You never used to get up until lunchtime, then you'd eat in the ship's dining room with all the men and they'd serve lovely Greek food, like the stuff I used to eat when I lived in Piraeus.

You didn't have to pay for your food. The men who were serving it just seemed to turn a blind eye to you. Most of them would have girls of their own on board anyway. During the day you could wander round the ship with your bloke and even watch television if you felt like it. You'd get another great meal at supper time and then at night there'd be as much drink and cigarettes as you wanted.

I always wanted quite a lot – not cigarettes, so much, but I used to knock back the booze. Even with all my experience I still needed a couple of double whiskies before I could climb into my bunk with a strange sailor, but it got easier as time went by. It was a bit like having regulars in London. After two weeks you got to know the blokes and sometimes you'd quite like them, so the next time the ship was in port you'd go with the same one. Some of the girls had relationships like this that had gone on for years.

After a couple of months I discovered that there was a better way of finding ships than just wandering around the docks looking at the flags, and I used to get hold of the daily shipping paper which told you which ships were coming in, when they would arrive and on which dock; this made life a lot easier.

One of the funny things for me about being on the ships, and something that I didn't expect, was that people still remembered me from when I'd been no. 1 stripper at the Glad-Ray Club. It was the dock workers, mostly, who recognized me. Often in the mornings when I came off the boats I'd hear shouts of 'Gloria, Gloria, get 'em off, gal!' and I'd put my head down and pretend it wasn't me. Somehow I felt uncomfortable at the thought that what I was doing might get back to Gladys, my boss at the Glad-Ray.

At any one time there'd often be 20 or 30 girls on a ship, so it was quite a big business that was operating, though as far as I know it wasn't organized by anyone outside and each girl was only working for herself. We used to chat to each other in the galley, which was where we ate and watched TV, about which ships we'd been on and which ones we were planning to visit next.

During the first week I was there one of the girls told me to make sure I had a check-up every two weeks in case of VD, because the sailors were really bad for that. I didn't need telling twice. She told me where the clinic was and although I was careful about making the men wear a Durex I still used to go for my fortnightly check-up just in case. The doctors at the clinic were good. They didn't tell you off, even though they knew what you were doing. One of them told me once that they preferred dealing with the girls who worked on the ships because they kept themselves clean and came for regular check-ups. It was the ones who just slept around with boys for fun – the amateurs, he called them – who got into worse trouble because they often didn't know they'd got VD until it was much too late and it had started doing damage. I felt almost respectable after he said that – it was as though if you slept with men as a profession you had a bit more status in the clinic than the girls who just gave it away.

Although the most common arrangement on the ships was the 'boyfriend' system it wasn't always the case. Sometimes, if they were the first ones on to a ship fresh into port, girls used to cash in on their scarcity value and find themselves a cabin where they could take paying customers like a conventional prostitute. I did business like that once on a Chinese ship. Usually Lizzie and I went on the ships together, but for some reason this time I was on my own and there were only a couple of other girls on board when I arrived. It soon became obvious from the attention I was getting that I had about six potential customers if I played my cards right and got going before the rest of the girls arrived. So I found myself a cabin with a bunk and started work.

All I thought when I started was that I'd make a quick few pounds before I went back to the canteen and started looking for a boyfriend. The problem was that after I'd been with the sixth customer a seventh came in, and then an eighth, and so it went on. They were coming off duty and when they found that the other girls still hadn't arrived they were queuing up outside my door.

The Chinese sailors were all very polite and incredibly clean, which made a change from some of the ships where they weren't too particular. The Chinese always filled a bowl of water and washed themselves before they'd go with you. I'd bought a box of condoms with me and it soon became like a production line. I didn't even take my dress off. I gave them two or three minutes each and when they'd finished I'd wash myself then lie back, clap my hands together and call for the next one – and the door would open to admit another one, often looking, to my eyes, exactly like the one who'd just left.

I charged them a fiver each and as I took each note I stuffed it down my bra for safe-keeping. After an hour-and-a-half I looked as if I had a 50-inch bust.

The only one of all the men I remember now is the ship's cook, and I only remember him because it was a disaster. He was on his second minute and I was making noises like you do to make them feel good when suddenly he stopped. Time was money. I said, 'What's the matter? What've you stopped for?' He said, 'Please. You are crying. Are you in pain? Am I hurting you?'

That was the end of that. I couldn't keep a straight face. On top of it being such a dumb question his equipment was the smallest I'd ever seen in my life.

When I called a halt after four hours, I was dizzy. I had been with nearly 60 men. No one I told about it afterwards believed it, but it was true. Looking back, I don't know why I did it except that when I started there were only six of them and when there got to be more than six there never seemed to be a good time to stop. As far as I know, maybe some of them had been back for a second or third time – it was all the same to me. Whatever the case, I staggered off the boat that night with nearly £300 in £5 notes stashed away inside my handbag.

I must have been working the boats for about four months when I had a bad row with Joyce. I was sad about it afterwards because we had always got on with each other since being kids and she'd been good to me by taking me in after I came back from Greece – though I was paying her rent while I was living with her, so I hadn't been taking advantage. I used to take her eldest girl Joycie with me on some of the ships sometimes when it was just an evening visit, though I didn't tell her what I was really doing. I used to leave her drinking orange juice or eating in the galley while she waited for me to finish seeing my 'boyfriend'.

Joyce herself knew what I was up to and I don't think she really approved, but after the time that Christmas when I'd cut my wrists she never talked about my being 'on the game' and when I was at home I kidded myself that she didn't mind.

The trouble happened because one of Joyce's kids, my little niece Carol, who was only about seven at the time, had said something rude to me – I think she'd called me a dirty tart. I don't suppose she even knew what it meant, but she said it in that cheeky way small girls are so good at and I blew my top. I said, 'Don't you talk to me like that, Carol! You'd better watch your mouth, girl, or I'll kill you.'

I over-reacted, I suppose, maybe because I was beginning to be ashamed of myself about what I was doing. But I must have frightened her and she started to cry, and when Joyce came in to see what was the matter Carol said that I'd hit her. It wasn't true. I hadn't touched her, but Joyce didn't believe me. She was livid and told me to leave.

I didn't argue. I packed my bags and went, but it hurt me that she took sides against me. Kids aren't always angels. She should have known that, and her little daughter had lied to her this time.

After that, everything seemed to go wrong. I found a room in a hotel near the docks with another girl off the ships called Mary and we carried on with our 'visiting', but my heart wasn't in it. What Carol had said had hit home. I loved kids. I'd spent most of my spare money on my sister's kids, on toys and clothes for them, and the thought, which had never occurred to me before, that they despised me for what I did began to prey on my mind. I realized that little Joycie must have guessed in the end what my trips to the ships were all about and she had obviously been talking to her sisters about me. Knowing that made me feel really bad.

The final straw came on Sunday afternoon when I was wandering around the docks with Mary. We were on the *Inca Capac* that week, but she was leaving soon and we needed another ship. I hadn't remembered to buy my shipping paper so we were looking up at the flags of the boats we passed to see where they were from. I remember I didn't have my glasses on so I could hardly see the ships themselves clearly, let alone the flags. We came to a big, modern-looking boat – we always preferred new ships because they were more comfortable – so I looked up to see if anyone was about. Suddenly I thought I saw someone move, so I waved like mad and shouted, 'Hello.' Mary looked at me as if she thought I'd gone mad.

'What are you waving at, Gloria?' she asked.

'That man there. Look, he's waving back at us,' I answered.

'Gloria, girl, that's a flag flapping,' she said. 'You're waving at a flag!'

I felt such a fool. My eyes had got so bad that I needed bifocals now, but vanity always made me leave them at home when I went on the ships. We were wandering along, rolling about, laughing to each other over my eyesight, when we came upon another ship. I don't know what nationality it was, but we knew it hadn't been in the previous night.

'Come on,' I said, 'let's try this one. Let's go up. Maybe we'll see someone. Maybe we'll get lucky.'

So we set off up the gangway. We didn't get very far, though. I'd taken three or four steps, that's all, and Mary was right behind me, when suddenly, seemingly out of nowhere, we were drenched with cold water. We looked up, gasping and spluttering, and saw some sailors standing on the deck above us. We stared up at them, trying to work out what had hit us, and as we watched they picked up a bucket of water and threw it over us. I couldn't believe it but then, as we stood there gaping up at them, a third shower of water hit us from the other side and a voice shouted, 'Clear off, you whores!'

We scarpered back down the gang-plank as fast as our legs would carry us and the voice followed us: 'Dirty bitches!' it called.

We were drenched to the skin. All my mascara was running into my eyes and my hair was plastered to my face. Mary was no better. We stood and looked at each other, speechless. I felt like an animal that someone had thrown out on to the street in disgrace. It was the only time anything like that had ever happened to me the whole time I was working the ships, though Mary said later she'd heard of it happening before on the docks. Coming as it did in the same week that Joyce's little girl had called me a dirty tart, it made me feel terrible.

I'd always got on pretty well with the men on the ships. It had never crossed my mind that some of them thought we were disgusting because of what we did. I used to kid myself that it was just like any other job of work and that's how the sailors saw it.

But I knew now what some of them – perhaps all of them – really thought, and I felt sick inside. I'd known the truth all along, really, but I'd pretended not to see it.

Neither of us wanted to go back to the *Inca Capac* looking like that, so we decided to go to our hotel instead. We called a taxi, and when the driver saw us looking like a couple of drowned rats he started laughing. 'What the hell happened to you two?' he asked.

We tried to make a joke out of it, but neither of us felt much like laughing.

Back at the hotel we sat on our beds and looked at each other.

'I thought they only threw buckets of water to stop dogs mating,' I said.

'Well, they called us bitches,' Mary answered, forcing a smile to her face.

We both giggled, but it didn't make us feel any better. Mary had been working the ships for about as long as I had and I could tell she was as upset as me.

'What are we going to do?' I asked her.

She shrugged her shoulders.

'I don't feel like going back after that,' she said, 'do you?'

I shook my head.

'I was getting fed up of it anyway,' I said. 'The novelty's worn off. It's time to do something else.'

It was Mary who came up with the idea.

'Why don't we go to Amsterdam?' she suggested.

The bell which always told me when an idea was good went 'ding' in my head. I'd heard about Amsterdam years ago from the girls in the Glad-Ray. They'd said they had great strip clubs there, the best in the world, and the money was the best too. I knew at once that Amsterdam was the answer.

So there, in a Liverpool hotel, I decided once and for all that I had come to the end of my days 'on the game'. I would go back to dancing and use my body for something I was good at and could be proud of doing. The one job in all my life so far which I'd really enjoyed was stripping. It seemed crazy to me now that I'd ever left it. I'd never enjoyed being a prostitute, so why on earth was I doing it? To get back at men for all the pain they'd given me? To repay Uncle John for raping me? I could see now that my reasoning was daft. The only person I was hurting was me – Gloria.

I knew that the time had finally come to put my childhood behind me. It hadn't been an easy time, but it was over. I wasn't going to let it spoil the rest of my life. I was grown-up now. It was time I stopped drifting and settled down to make a career for myself. Stripping might not be most people's idea of a 'respectable' profession but I wasn't ashamed of it and that was what mattered.

I turned to Mary, my mind made up.

'Right then, Amsterdam it is,' I said, and she laughed and threw me my suitcase. Together we started to pack.

19

All that happened a long time ago now. It's eleven years since Mary and I left Liverpool for Holland, but I've stood by the promise I made to myself that night in the hotel and I never went back on the game.

It felt as though I had come out of a long, dark tunnel after I made that decision, and life started to get better almost straight away. In Holland I got to be no. 1 stripper at the Casa Rosso Club, the most famous club in Amsterdam – no half measures for Gloria – and stayed there for seven years. Somehow I stopped being so restless once I'd sorted myself out. I can't say there weren't any rough patches, but on the whole I had a ball after leaving Liverpool. In between seasons at the Casa Rosso I travelled to America, Africa and over most of Europe. I used to be really jealous of the girls I went to school with at Hoole Secondary Modern because they had so many advantages over me and yet I bet that in the end I've done more things and seen more of the world than any of them.

But the best part was still to come. In 1983 I took a working holiday in Greece and met and fell in love with a boy called Costa Micailidis. We were married in Liverpool six months after we met, and for the first time in my life I found myself with someone who wasn't frightened by the amount of love I had to give but gave me back just as much in return.

No one would call me religious, but I often think it was some sort of destiny that brought Costa and me together. It sounds corny to say you were made for each other, but that's the only way it feels. We understand each other so well, despite our different backgrounds, that sometimes it's frightening. It's as though there's a kind of telepathy between us and we often know what the other one is thinking without anything being said.

Costa knows all about my past and he accepts it. He's never blamed me for what I did as other people have, and I know now that whatever happens to me in the future I'll have someone on my side. I won't be fighting on my own, and that's a good feeling.

We've lived in Liverpool since we've been married, first in a rented room and now in a housing trust flat. I never went back to stripping once I met Costa. I just didn't want to do it any more, although it had given me a great life for seven years. I didn't think it would be fair to him.

It's not been easy. There's no work in Liverpool for either of us, but starting my married life here was like coming home. I felt I belonged. To keep myself busy I work in a charity shop six days a week, selling secondhand clothes to raise money for cystic fibrosis. Quite a reformed character, you might say!

A funny thing happened the other day. A Chinese woman walked into the charity shop and I noticed her staring at me. Finally she came up to the counter.

'Is it you, Gloria?' she asked.

It was Susan, one of the girls who'd run away with me on our Great Escape from the children's home. She told me she was helping run her father's fish-and-chip shop now, which turned out to be just round the corner from our flat. We talked for ages, reminding each other of all the things that had happened to us all those years before. It was the first time I had ever met any of the other girls who had been at the home with me and the first time I'd really talked about what happened there to someone who knew what it was like. And when at last she went, promising to keep in touch, I felt really happy. It was as though a ghost had finally been laid to rest.

I don't think you can ever turn your back on your past and shut it out. The things in my past happened to me. They made me what I am and there's no way I'm ever going to be able to forget them or pretend they didn't happen. But I've learned one big lesson over these last eleven years, and that's self-respect – I know that the important thing for me, Gloria, is to accept and like myself for what I am now, not what I was, and that, from day to day, is what I try to do.